Business Tax

(Finance Act 2023)

Tutorial

for assessments from 29 January 2024

Aubrey Penning
Bob Thomas

Published by Osborne Books Limited
Tel 01905 748071
Email books@osbornebooks.co.uk
Website www.osbornebooks.co.uk

Design by Laura Ingham

Printed by CPI Group (UK) Limited, Croydon, CR0 4YY, on environmentally friendly, acid-free paper from managed forests.

British Library Cataloguing in Publication Data
A catalogue record for this book is available from the British Library

ISBN 978-1-911681-07-6

Contents

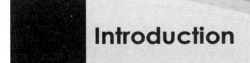

Introduction

Qualifications covered

This book has been written specifically to cover the Unit 'Business Tax' which is optional for the following qualifications:

AAT Level 4 Diploma in Professional Accounting

AAT Diploma in Professional Accounting – SCQF Level 8

The book contains a clear text with worked examples and case studies, chapter summaries and key terms to help with revision. Each chapter concludes with a wide range of activities, many in the style of AAT computer based assessments.

Osborne Study and Revision Materials

Additional materials, tailored to the needs of students studying this unit and revising for the assessment, include:

- **Workbooks:** paperback books with practice activities and exams
- **Student Zone:** access to Osborne Books online resources
- **Osborne Books App:** Osborne Books ebooks for mobiles and tablets

Visit www.osbornebooks.co.uk for details of study and revision resources and access to online material.

Exams, Finance Acts and tax years

This book has been designed to include guidance and exercises based on Tax Year 2023/24 (Finance Act 2023). We understand that the AAT plans to assess this legislation from 29 January 2024 to January 2025. Tutors and students are advised to check the dates with the AAT and ensure that they sit the correct computer based assessment.

Tax data

NATIONAL INSURANCE

Tax Year 2023/24

Self-employed National Insurance contributions (sole traders and partners)

Class 2 contributions are payable at a flat rate of £3.45 per week (unless below the 'small profits threshold'), and in addition,

Class 4 contributions are payable on the profits as follows:

9% of profits for the year between £12,570 and £50,270, plus

2% of profits above £50,270

CORPORATION TAX

Profits	Financial Year 2022 (ie 1/4/2022 – 31/3/2023)	Financial Year 2023 (ie 1/4/2023 – 31/3/2024
£0 - £50,000		Small profits rate 19%
£50,001 - £250,000	Main Rate 19%	Main rate 25% less marginal relief
over 250,000		Main rate 25%

Marginal relief 3/200 x (upper limit – TTP)

INCOME TAX

Personal Allowance for tax year 2023/24: £12,570

Tax bands 2023/24

(General Income)

	£
Basic rate 20%	0 – 37,700
Higher rate 40%	37,701 to 125,140
Additional rate 45%	over 125,140

CAPITAL GAINS TAX – FOR INDIVIDUALS

	2023/24
Annual Exempt Amount	£6,000

Rates

Gains	10% and/or 20%
	(10% where business asset disposal relief is claimed)

Note – further tax data is available in the AAT reference material reproduced at the end of this book.

RETAIL PRICE INDEX (for indexation allowance for companies only)

	Jan	Feb	Mar	Apr	May	Jun	Jul	Aug	Sept	Oct	Nov	Dec
2017	265.5	268.4	269.3	270.6	271.7	272.3	272.9	274.7	275.1	275.3	275.8	278.1
2016	258.8	260.0	261.1	261.4	262.1	263.1	263.4	264.4	264.9	264.8	265.5	267.1
2015	255.4	256.7	257.1	258.0	258.5	258.9	258.6	259.8	259.6	259.5	259.8	260.6
2014	252.6	254.2	254.8	255.7	255.9	256.3	256.0	257.0	257.6	257.7	257.1	257.5
2013	245.8	247.6	248.7	249.5	250.0	249.7	249.7	251.0	251.9	251.9	252.1	253.4
2012	238.0	239.9	240.8	242.5	242.4	241.8	242.1	243.0	244.2	245.6	245.6	246.8
2011	229.0	231.3	232.5	234.4	235.2	235.2	234.7	236.1	237.9	238.0	238.5	239.4
2010	218.0	219.2	220.7	222.8	223.6	224.1	223.6	224.5	225.3	225.8	226.8	228.4
2009	210.1	211.4	211.3	211.5	212.8	213.4	213.4	214.4	215.3	216.0	216.6	218.0
2008	209.8	211.4	212.2	214.0	215.1	216.8	216.5	217.2	218.4	217.7	216.0	212.9
2007	201.6	203.1	204.4	205.4	206.2	207.3	206.1	207.3	208.0	208.9	209.7	210.9
2006	193.4	194.2	195.0	196.5	197.7	198.5	198.5	199.2	200.1	200.4	201.8	202.7
2005	188.9	189.6	190.5	191.6	192.0	192.0	192.2	192.6	193.1	193.3	193.6	194.1
2004	183.1	183.8	184.6	185.7	186.5	186.8	186.8	187.4	188.1	188.6	189.0	189.9
2003	178.4	179.3	179.9	181.2	181.5	181.3	181.3	181.6	182.5	182.6	182.7	183.5
2002	173.3	173.8	174.5	175.7	176.2	176.2	175.9	176.4	177.6	177.9	178.2	178.5
2001	171.1	172.0	172.2	173.1	174.2	174.4	173.3	174.0	174.6	174.3	173.6	173.4
2000	166.6	167.5	168.4	170.1	170.7	171.1	170.5	170.5	171.7	171.6	172.1	172.2
1999	163.4	163.7	164.1	165.2	165.6	165.6	165.1	165.5	166.2	166.5	166.7	167.3
1998	159.5	160.3	160.8	162.6	163.5	163.4	163.0	163.7	164.4	164.5	164.4	164.4
1997	154.4	155.0	155.4	156.3	156.9	157.5	157.5	158.5	159.3	159.5	159.6	160.0
1996	150.2	150.9	151.5	152.6	152.9	153.0	152.4	153.1	153.8	153.8	153.9	154.4
1995	146.0	146.9	147.5	149.0	149.6	149.8	149.1	149.9	150.6	149.8	149.8	150.7
1994	141.3	142.1	142.5	144.2	144.7	144.7	144.0	144.7	145.0	145.2	145.3	146.0
1993	137.9	138.8	139.3	140.6	141.1	141.0	140.7	141.3	141.9	141.8	141.6	141.9
1992	135.6	136.3	136.7	138.8	139.3	139.3	138.8	138.9	139.4	139.9	139.7	139.2
1991	130.2	130.9	131.4	133.1	133.5	134.1	133.8	134.1	134.6	135.1	135.6	135.7

	Jan	Feb	Mar	Apr	May	Jun	Jul	Aug	Sept	Oct	Nov	Dec
1990	119.50	120.20	121.40	125.10	126.20	126.70	126.80	128.10	129.30	130.30	130.00	129.90
1989	111.00	111.80	112.30	114.30	115.00	115.40	115.50	115.80	116.60	117.50	118.50	118.80
1988	103.30	103.70	104.10	105.80	106.20	106.60	106.70	107.90	108.40	109.50	110.00	110.30
1987	100.00	100.40	100.60	101.80	101.90	101.90	101.80	102.10	102.40	102.90	103.40	103.30
1986	96.25	96.60	96.73	97.67	97.85	97.79	97.52	97.82	98.30	98.45	99.29	99.62
1985	91.20	91.94	92.80	94.78	95.21	95.41	95.23	95.49	95.44	95.59	95.92	96.05
1984	86.84	87.20	87.48	88.64	88.97	89.20	89.10	89.94	90.11	90.67	90.95	90.87
1983	82.61	82.97	83.12	84.28	84.64	84.84	85.30	85.68	86.06	86.36	86.67	86.89
1982	-	-	79.44	81.04	81.62	81.85	81.88	81.90	81.85	82.26	82.66	82.51

1 Introduction to business taxation

this chapter covers...

In this chapter we provide a brief review of the various types of UK tax that apply to businesses and are studied in this book. Corporation Tax is payable by limited companies, while sole traders and partnerships are subject to Income Tax. We will also look at the role of HM Revenue & Customs, and see how sources of law relate to tax.

We will briefly look at how tax computations for both Corporation Tax and Income Tax work, before examining how income is divided up into categories for these taxes.

We need to understand how income and profits are taxed under these two taxes, and we will examine the impact of financial years and tax years on the calculation and reporting of tax. This includes a study of the way that tax returns work and when they need to be submitted by and the payment dates of tax.

Next we will learn how National Insurance is calculated for the self-employed and those in partnership.

Finally we will examine the responsibilities of the tax practitioner, including those relating to confidentiality and record keeping.

WHAT IS 'BUSINESS TAX'?

The 'business tax' that we are going to study in this book is not a single tax, but instead is a number of UK taxes that have an impact on businesses.

The specific taxes that affect any business in the UK will depend primarily on the legal structure of the business. You will probably be aware from your accounting studies of the three main ways (listed below) that businesses can be formed. We are going to examine the tax situation for:

- limited companies

- sole traders, and

- partnerships

Limited companies (whether public or private) are incorporated bodies and therefore have their own legal existence that is quite separate from that of the owners. The profits that limited companies generate are subject to **Corporation Tax**.

Sole traders and **partnerships** are both unincorporated businesses, which means that there is no legal separation between the owner(s) of the business and the business itself. For this reason the profits from these businesses are dealt with under **Income Tax**, where they are assessed directly in relation to the business owners – the sole trader or partners. This is the same Income Tax that most of us pay on our income from employment or savings. If you have studied the Unit 'Personal Tax', you will have seen how Income Tax works in some detail. To succeed in the 'Business Tax' Unit you only have to understand the impact of Income Tax on business profits.

In the first part of this book we will be examining how Corporation Tax works, and how we can calculate how much Corporation Tax limited companies should pay. To do this we will need to work out the amount of trading profits that are subject to Corporation Tax. We will also need to work out the chargeable gains that result from the disposal of certain assets, and incorporate this along with other company profits in the Corporation Tax computation.

In the second part of the book we will be looking at how the profits of sole traders and partnerships are assessed under Income Tax. We will also see how Capital Gains Tax can affect these business owners if they dispose of certain business assets.

We will also look at the impact of National Insurance on the self-employed and those in partnerships, and learn how to calculate the amounts that need to be paid.

The table on the opposite page shows the topics we will study in this Unit. The content of the Unit 'Personal Tax' is also shown for comparison. There are other taxes, such as Value Added Tax and Inheritance Tax, which affect businesses, but they are beyond the requirements of your studies here and so are not covered in this book.

THE TAX SYSTEM

We will first look at the background to the way that the tax system works. We will then outline the way in which numerical tax calculations are carried out.

HM Revenue & Customs

Income Tax, Corporation Tax and Capital Gains Tax are all administered by HM Revenue & Customs, which also collects National Insurance Contributions and VAT. This is a government organisation that has an administrative structure containing the following three parts:

- taxpayer service offices are the main offices that individual taxpayers deal with, and handle much of the basic Income Tax assessment and collection functions
- taxpayer district offices deal with Corporation Tax and more complex Income Tax issues
- tax enquiry centres deal with enquiries and provide forms and leaflets to taxpayers

These three functions are located in offices throughout the UK. In smaller centres some functions may be combined into one office, while in larger towns and cities they may be located separately.

the law governing tax – statute law

The authority to levy taxes comes from two sources. The first is legislation passed by Parliament, known as statute law. You may have heard of the Finance Acts. These are generally published each year and give details of any changes to taxes. These changes will have been proposed by the Chancellor of the Exchequer (usually in the budget) and passed by Parliament. In this book we will be using information from the Finance Act 2023, which relates to the financial year 2023 for companies and the tax year 2023/24 for individuals.

We will see exactly what is meant by financial years and tax years later in this chapter. There are also other relevant statute laws that were designed to create frameworks for the way that certain taxes work.

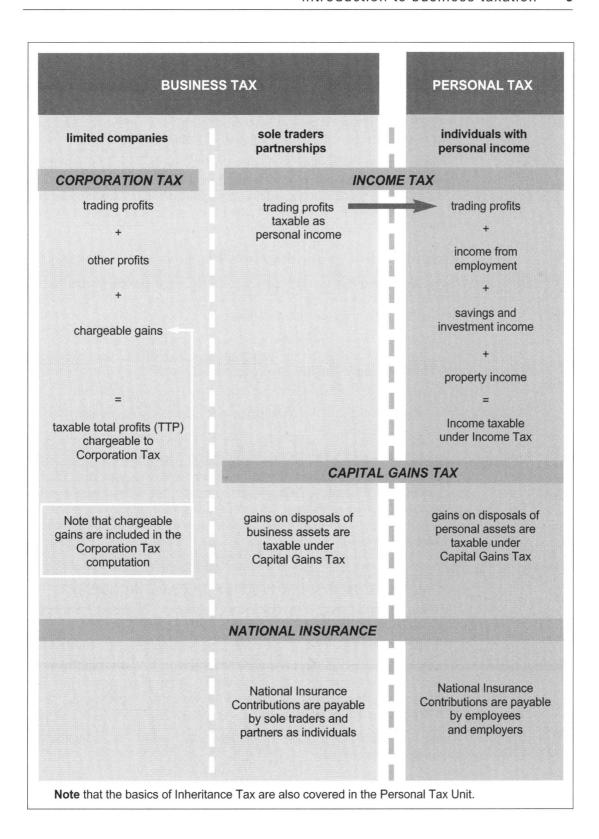

BUSINESS TAX

PERSONAL TAX

limited companies

sole traders partnerships

individuals with personal income

CORPORATION TAX

INCOME TAX

trading profits

+

other profits

+

chargeable gains

=

taxable total profits (TTP) chargeable to Corporation Tax

Note that chargeable gains are included in the Corporation Tax computation

trading profits taxable as personal income

trading profits

+

income from employment

+

savings and investment income

+

property income

=

Income taxable under Income Tax

CAPITAL GAINS TAX

gains on disposals of business assets are taxable under Capital Gains Tax

gains on disposals of personal assets are taxable under Capital Gains Tax

NATIONAL INSURANCE

National Insurance Contributions are payable by sole traders and partners as individuals

National Insurance Contributions are payable by employees and employers

Note that the basics of Inheritance Tax are also covered in the Personal Tax Unit.

the law governing tax – case law

The second source of tax law is called **'case law'**, and draws its authority from decisions taken in court cases. Taxation can be very complicated, and sometimes disagreements between HM Revenue & Customs and taxpayers result in court cases. The final outcome of such cases can then become 'case law' and influences future interpretation of statute law.

Although there is a substantial amount of statute law and case law that is relevant to the taxation of businesses in the UK, this book will try to keep references to specific law to a minimum. While it will be important to know the rules that apply to certain situations, you will not be required to quote from the legislation or cases in your examination.

information available from HM Revenue & Customs

In addition to the tax law outlined above, there are interpretations and explanations of various issues that are published by HM Revenue & Customs. The main ones are as follows:

- extra-statutory concessions are issued when HM Revenue & Customs agrees to impose a less strict interpretation of the law than would otherwise apply in particular circumstances

- HM Revenue & Customs statements of practice are public announcements of how HM Revenue & Customs interprets specific rules

- Guides and Help Sheets are issued to help taxpayers complete the necessary return forms and calculate their tax

A large array of publications and forms can be downloaded from the HM Revenue & Customs website at www.gov.uk. This website also provides data on Corporation Tax and Income Tax rates for a range of tax years. You will find it useful to have a look at what is available on this site when you have an opportunity.

CALCULATION OF CORPORATION TAX AND INCOME TAX

Corporation Tax

In Chapters 2 to 5 in this book we will be looking in some detail about the way in which Corporation Tax is calculated. At this point we will just show how the system works in outline, by using a simple format for a **Corporation Tax computation**.

We will then use a numerical example that reflects a straightforward situation for a company.

an outline Corporation Tax computation		
		£
	Trading Profits	X
+	Income from Investments	X
+	Chargeable Gains	X
=	Taxable Total Profits (TTP)	X
	Corporation Tax on TTP	X

A simple Corporation Tax computation would look like this if we assume the following figures:

Corporation Tax Computation for AB Company Limited for year ended 31/3/2024	
	£
Trading Profits	1,300,000
Income from Investments	400,000
Chargeable Gains	300,000
Taxable Total Profits (TTP)	2,000,000
Corporation Tax on TTP (£2,000,000 × 25%)	500,000

Income Tax

In the later chapters in this book we will be looking at how trading profits are assessed under Income Tax. Although we will not need to use a full Income Tax computation in this Unit, we will now just briefly see how it will appear. This is so that you can envisage how the trading profit figures would be used to work out Income Tax.

an outline Income Tax computation

		£
	Income – earnings and other income	X
	Less personal allowance	(X)
=	Taxable income	X
	Tax payable on taxable income	X

A simple Income Tax computation for a sole trader might appear as follows:

Income Tax Computation

	£
Trading Profits	15,000
Other General Income	1,000
	16,000
less Personal Allowance	12,570
Taxable income	3,430
Tax payable at 20%*	686

*Other rates of Income Tax can also apply.

HOW INCOME IS CATEGORISED FOR TAX PURPOSES

The income that a company or an individual receives is divided into categories, depending on what sort of income it is and where it comes from. These categories apply to both Corporation Tax and Income Tax, and are based on descriptions of income. This is done so that:

- the correct rules on how to work out the income are used (since these vary with the categories), and

- the correct rates of tax are used (since they can also depend on the type of income when applying Income Tax)

When studying this Unit we will only need to know the outline detail of most of these categories, because we will be mainly concentrating on trading income. The list and descriptions shown below have been simplified to include only the categories that you need to know about in this Unit. It does not include, for example, the categories that relate to overseas income.

'Property Income' – Rental income from land and property

'Trading Income' – Profits of trades and professions

'Savings & Investment Income' – UK Interest

FINANCIAL YEARS AND TAX YEARS

Corporation Tax – financial years

The rates of Corporation Tax are changed from time to time (normally in the Chancellor's budget) and relate to specific **financial years**. These years run from 1 April in one calendar year to 31 March in the following year. The year that runs from 1 April 2023 to 31 March 2024 is known as the financial year 2023 – in other words, the financial year is named after the calendar year that most of it falls into.

Income Tax – tax years

For Income Tax purposes time is divided into **tax years** (sometimes called **fiscal years**). Individuals' income and Income Tax is worked out separately for each tax year. The tax year runs from 6 April in one calendar year to 5 April in the next calendar year. The tax year running from 6 April 2023 to 5 April 2024 would be described as the 2023/24 tax year.

HOW TAX RETURNS WORK

A **Tax Return** is a document issued by HM Revenue & Customs and used to collect information about a company's or an individual's income and gains. The Company Tax Return (the CT600 form) is used to collect information for Corporation Tax purposes, whereas the tax return for individuals provides data relating to Income Tax and Capital Gains Tax. Both companies and individuals are subject to the **self-assessment** system of tax. This means that they declare their profits and other taxable income on the tax return, and can then pay their own tax without HM Revenue & Customs sending them a bill. Individuals who submit a paper-based return within a certain deadline can ask HM Revenue & Customs to work the tax out for them, but otherwise the taxpayer (company or individual) or their agent must calculate the tax. Where the Income Tax return is submitted online, the tax is calculated automatically.

tax returns for limited companies

A company must submit a CT600 form for every **Chargeable Accounting Period** (CAP). Provided the accounts are produced for a period of twelve months or less, the company's normal accounting period will be the same as the CAP. Longer accounting periods are divided into two CAPs, one based on the first twelve months of the accounting period, and the other based on the remainder of the period. We will look at the practicalities of dividing up the figures for a long accounting period later in the book.

Note that the company tax return relates to the company's Chargeable Accounting Period, not a particular financial year. The form sets out the information that is needed by HM Revenue & Customs, and provides a standard format for calculations. It must be submitted within twelve months after the end of the company's accounting period from which the CAP was derived, or three months after the 'notice to deliver a tax return' has been issued, if later. All companies must file returns online.

Note that the term **'accounting period' (AP)** can also be used to describe a Chargeable Accounting Period (CAP). The AAT reference material (which is reproduced in the appendix to this book) takes this approach.

tax returns for individuals

Individuals with complex tax affairs (including all those in business as sole traders or partners) need to complete a separate tax return for each tax year. Note that individuals' tax returns relate to tax years, not accounting periods. The basis of assessment for trading income for individuals and partnerships is the profit arising in the tax year. If the accounting period is aligned with the tax year (eg year ending 5/4/24) then the profits of the accounting period will be used in the tax return. An accounting year end of 31 March is treated as equivalent to a year end of 5 April. If the accounting periods do not align with the tax year, then apportionment of the profits of accounting periods will be necessary.

This 'tax year' basis of assessment relates to 2023/24 onwards, and it is significantly different to the previous 'current year' basis. There are special transitional arrangements in place for existing sole traders and partnerships, but you do not need to be aware of these arrangements for your studies.

scheduling of the income tax return

Individuals and partnerships can submit their tax returns either in the traditional paper format, or online. HMRC is encouraging the use of online submissions, and has introduced the following different deadlines for each method of tax return submission:

- submission of paper-based tax returns must be made by the 31 October following the end of the tax year. This means that the

2023/24 return would need to be submitted by 31 October 2024. If required, HMRC will calculate the tax relating to a properly completed return if it meets this deadline

- submission of an online return can be made at any time up to 31 January following the end of the tax year. The amount of tax is automatically calculated by the computer program once the online form has been completed, and the taxpayer can print out a copy for their records. An online return for the tax year 2023/24 would therefore need to be submitted by 31 January 2025

WHEN TO PAY TAX

The payment dates for companies and individuals differ, so we will examine them separately.

companies – Corporation Tax

We saw in the last section that company tax returns are completed for each Chargeable Accounting Period (CAP). Unless instalment payments are necessary, the Corporation Tax that has been calculated is normally payable nine months and one day after the end of the Chargeable Accounting Period that it relates to. For example, the Corporation Tax relating to the Chargeable Accounting Period 1/1/2023 to 31/12/2023 will normally be payable on 1/10/2024. If the period falls into more than one financial year, this will be taken account of in the tax calculation (if necessary) but it does not affect the payment date. The payment date relates only to the period, not to the financial year.

If a company is 'large', then it will pay most of its Corporation Tax earlier in instalments, with only the final amount falling due on the date referred to above. A 'large' company is one with profits over £1,500,000 for a 12 month CAP. Where a company has one or more associated companies, then the limit of £1,500,000 is divided by the number of associated companies plus one. For example, a company with two associated companies would be 'large' if its profits were over £1,500,000 / 3 = £500,000.

For 'large' companies that exceed the limit, all of the company's estimated Corporation Tax liability must be paid in the following four instalments (25% in each instalment). The first instalment is due on day 14 of month seven within the CAP. The next three instalments follow at three monthly intervals. Any remaining balance of Corporation Tax (since the instalments were based on an estimate) will be payable at the normal due date, nine months and one day after the end of the CAP. Estimates should be revised each quarter if necessary.

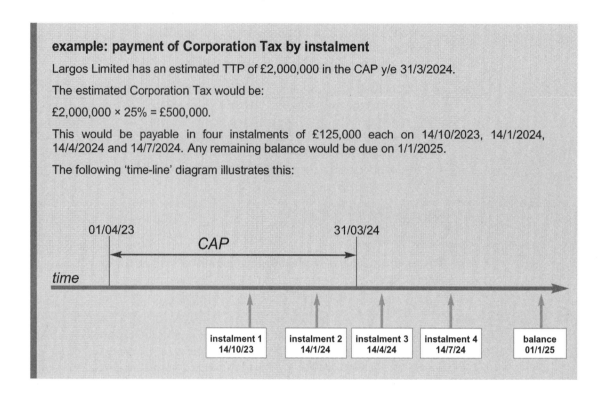

example: payment of Corporation Tax by instalment

Largos Limited has an estimated TTP of £2,000,000 in the CAP y/e 31/3/2024.

The estimated Corporation Tax would be:

£2,000,000 × 25% = £500,000.

This would be payable in four instalments of £125,000 each on 14/10/2023, 14/1/2024, 14/4/2024 and 14/7/2024. Any remaining balance would be due on 1/1/2025.

The following 'time-line' diagram illustrates this:

Notice that for companies, the payment of tax is due before the final filing date for the tax return. This means that the tax calculation will have to have been carried out by the payment date (so that the payment amount is known), even though the actual form need not be submitted until nearly three months later! The return can always be submitted early if desired.

individuals – Income Tax

For income from trading profits, there is no system set up to automatically deduct Income Tax as there is for employees. The outstanding balance of Income Tax that relates to business profits and other income from which tax has not been deducted will need to be paid to HM Revenue & Customs according to the following rules:

The *final* date for payment of the Income Tax that relates to a tax year is the 31 January *following the end of that tax year*.

For some taxpayers there may also be payments on account that must be made before the final date. These are due as follows:

- first payment on account is due on 31 January within the tax year

- second payment on account is due on 31 July following the end of the tax year

For the tax year 2023/24 the payment dates would be:

> 31 January 2024 for the first payment on account,
>
> 31 July 2024 for the second payment on account, and
>
> 31 January 2025 for the final payment

The two payments on account are calculated as follows:

Each payment on account is based on **half** the Income Tax and NIC amount due for the **previous** year (after deducting tax paid under PAYE and other Income Tax deducted at source).

Suppose, for example, that a partner only had trading income, and no other income. If his Income Tax and Class 4 NIC liability for 2022/23 was £7,000, none of this would have been paid by deduction at source.

This means that for 2023/24 he would need to make two payments on account. Each of the two payments on account would be:

$1/2 \times £7,000 = £3,500$.

These payments on account for 2023/24 would be made on 31/1/24 and 31/7/24. If the Income Tax amount for each year is quite similar, there would not be much left to pay (or have refunded) on the final date of 31/1/25.

Payments on account do not have to be made if either:

- the amount of tax payable the previous year was less than £1,000 (excluding tax deducted at source), or
- more than 80% of the tax due the previous year was collected at source

Payments on account can also be reduced or eliminated if the taxpayer makes a claim that his tax for the coming year will be less than for the previous year.

Notice that when payments on account are required, two payments will be due on each 31 January. For example, on 31 January 2024 there would be due both:

> the final payment for the tax year 2022/23, and
>
> the first payment on account for the tax year 2023/24

We saw earlier that 31 January following the tax year was also the final date for submitting an online tax return, so for Income Tax these two dates coincide.

The table on the next page illustrates the main points relating to tax returns and payment dates.

Companies	Individuals (Sole Traders and Partnerships)
Corporation Tax	**Income Tax**
Company Tax Return (CT600) includes taxation of Corporation Tax for Chargeable Accounting Period (CAP).	Tax return includes supplementary pages for sole traders and partners, and relates to tax year.
Return submitted online by 12 months after end of period that accounts are based on.	Paper return submitted by 31 Oct following tax year, or online return submitted by 31 Jan following tax year.
Final payment by nine months and one day after end of CAP.	Final payment by 31 Jan following tax year.
Large companies also make earlier instalment payments.	Many taxpayers also make two payments on account.

Case Study

DIVERSE ACCOUNTING PRACTICE: TAX RETURNS

It is August 2023. You are a trainee employed by the Diverse Accounting Practice, working in its Tax Department. The practice uses online submission for all tax returns. You are currently scheduling work related to two clients as follows:

The Mammoth Company Limited produces annual accounts to the 31 January. The accounts for the year ended 31/1/2023 have been completed and are awaiting the necessary tax work.

Jo Small is a sole trader who has been trading for many years. The practice has produced accounts for her for the year ended 31/3/2024.

required

State the type of tax return that will need to be completed for each of the clients. Explain how each return is related to the client's accounting period, and the latest submission dates for the returns. State the final date for the payment of outstanding tax after any instalments or payments on account have been made.

solution

The Mammoth Company Limited will require a company tax return (form CT600). This will relate to the Chargeable Accounting Period (CAP) 1/2/2022 to 31/1/2023. The form must be submitted online by 12 months after the end of the accounting period – 31/1/2024. The final Corporation Tax payment must be made by 1/11/2023 (nine months and one day after the end of the CAP).

Jo Small will need a tax return for the tax year 2023/24. The accounting period of year ended 31/3/2024 will be assessed in this tax year. The main part of the form will need to be completed, along with the supplementary pages relating to self-employment. The online tax return must be submitted by 31/1/2025. The final Income Tax payment relating to 2023/24 will also have to be made by 31/1/2025.

NATIONAL INSURANCE

If you are an employee, you are probably familiar with employee National Insurance Contributions (NIC), which are deducted through Pay-As-You-Earn, along with Income Tax. In our study of business tax we will be looking at National Insurance Contributions, payable by self-employed individuals (sole traders and partners) in respect of their own profits.

self-employed National Insurance Contributions

There are two classes of NIC that apply to both sole traders and partners.

- **Class 2 contributions** are payable at a flat rate of £3.45 per week (unless the profits are below the 'small profits threshold' – see below), and, in addition,

- **Class 4 contributions** are payable on profits above £12,570 per year

The profits for self-employed NIC purposes are the same ones that are used for Income Tax purposes – the assessable trading profits. Where profits are less than £6,725 (2023/24) then the small profits threshold means that Class 2 contributions need not be paid.

Neither Class 2 nor Class 4 NIC is payable by those either under 16 years of age or over pensionable age at the start of the tax year.

The rates for Class 4 contributions for 2023/24 are:

- 9% of profits for the year between £12,570 and £50,270, plus

- 2% of profits above £50,270

If profits are below £12,570 then there are no Class 4 contributions.

---

example – NI for the self-employed

Sonita is a sole trader with trading profits of £60,000 in 2023/24.

Her NIC liability for the year would be:

		£	£
Class 2 contributions:	£3.45 × 52 =		179.40
Class 4 contributions:	(£50,270 – £12,570) × 9% =	3,393.00	
	plus		
	(£60,000 – £50,270) × 2% =	194.60	
			3,587.60
			3,767.00

Both Class 2 and Class 4 contributions are calculated at the same time as Income Tax under the self-assessment system, and entered on the tax return and paid along with the Income Tax for the year. Class 4 contributions are included in any calculation of payment on account, but Class 2 are not.

TAX PLANNING, TAX AVOIDANCE AND TAX EVASION

Tax planning involves looking at an individual's or a company's financial planning from a tax perspective. The purpose of tax planning is to see how to accomplish all the other elements of the financial plan in the most tax-efficient manner, and so minimise tax. Tax planning should only involve legal and ethical methods of minimising the tax liability.

It is important to distinguish between the practice of tax avoidance, which may be legal, and tax evasion, which is illegal. Tax avoidance involves using legitimate tax rules and allowances to minimise the amount of tax that is due. This could include an individual investing in ISAs so that any interest received is tax-free.

Tax evasion involves using illegal methods to escape paying the correct amount of tax. Examples would include entering false information in a tax return, or failing to notify HMRC about a taxable source of income on which tax has not been paid. Those who carry out tax evasion risk criminal prosecution.

While tax avoidance and tax evasion may appear to be easily distinguishable at each end of the scale, there will always be situations that may not be so clear cut. In particular, some 'tax avoidance schemes' have been developed that may not be legal.

HMRC has stated that where a scheme relies **on concealment, pretence, non-disclosure** or **misrepresentation** of the true facts then this is illegal tax evasion.

The government has developed various ways that it hopes to prevent so-called 'aggressive' tax avoidance schemes. Tax avoidance schemes need to be disclosed to HMRC, who will then investigate the schemes to ensure that they are legal. HMRC has stated that using a tax avoidance scheme marks the individual out as a high-risk taxpayer, and that this will lead to close scrutiny of all their tax affairs, not just those involving the tax avoidance scheme.

In 2013 legislation was introduced to outlaw some schemes that were deemed to be 'abusive'. This legislation is known as the 'General Anti-Abuse Rule' (GAAR). It is based on the rejection of the old approach taken by the Courts that taxpayers are free to use their ingenuity to reduce their tax bills by any lawful means, however contrived those means might be.

In broad terms, the GAAR outlaws action taken by a taxpayer to achieve a favourable tax result that Parliament **did not anticipate** when it introduced the tax rules in question, where that course of action cannot '**reasonably be regarded as reasonable**'.

This 'double reasonableness test' sets a high threshold for HMRC to prove that an arrangement is abusive and therefore illegal.

Aggressive tax avoidance schemes are certainly unethical and rely on taxpayers not paying their fair share of tax.

The key to using legal tax avoidance measures is to only use tax rules in the way that they were originally intended by Parliament. So the use of ISAs to avoid paying tax on savings interest is entirely proper, since it is in line with the original intention of the legislation.

In general, anyone who suspects that tax evasion is being carried out is advised to report this to HMRC. This can be done anonymously. HMRC advises the person reporting not to attempt to discover any more information about the suspected tax evasion, and not to tell anyone else.

In the next section we will see how the AAT code of professional ethics deals with situations where a client is suspected of tax evasion. It is important that the code is followed in these circumstances.

THE DUTIES AND RESPONSIBILITIES OF A TAX PRACTITIONER

A person who acts as a professional by helping clients (either companies or individuals) with their tax affairs has responsibilities:

- to the client, and
- to HM Revenue & Customs

The AAT has published a revised **Code of Professional Ethics** that deals with these and other issues. This applies to both AAT students and members, and the document can be downloaded from the website www.aat.org.uk.

A summary of the duties and responsibilities outlined by the AAT is as follows:

- maintain client confidentiality
- adopt an ethical approach and maintain an objective outlook
- give timely and constructive advice to clients
- conduct themselves honestly and professionally with HMRC

A tax advisor is liable to a penalty if they assist in making an incorrect return.

confidentiality

Keeping a client's or customer's dealings confidential is an essential element of professional ethics. As far as confidentiality for a tax practitioner is concerned, the Code referred to above states that confidentiality should always be observed, unless either:

- authority has been given to disclose the information (by the client), or
- there is a legal or professional right or duty to disclose

The Code also says that:

'Information about a past, present, or prospective client's or employer's affairs, or the affairs of clients of employers, acquired in a work context is likely to be confidential if it is not a matter of public knowledge.'

The rules of confidentiality apply in a social environment as well as a business one, and care should be taken to not inadvertently disclose confidential information. The need to comply also extends after a business relationship has ended – for example, if there was a change of employment.

One important exception to the normal rules of confidentiality is where 'money laundering' is known or suspected. 'Money laundering' includes any process of concealing or disguising the proceeds of any criminal offence, including tax evasion.

Where a practitioner has knowledge or suspicion that his client is money laundering, then he has a duty to inform the relevant person or authority. For those in a group practice this would be the Money Laundering Reporting Officer (MLRO), and for a sole practitioner the National Crime Agency (NCA).

It is an offence to warn the client that a report of this type is going to be made about him. Money laundering therefore is not a situation where authority would be sought from the client to disclose information!

taxation services

The Code states the following regarding taxation services:

'A member providing professional tax services has a duty to put forward the best position in favour of a client or an employer. However, the service must be carried out with professional competence, must not in any way impair integrity or objectivity, and must be consistent with the law.'

The Code also states that:

'A member shall only undertake taxation work on the basis of full disclosure by the client or employer. The member, in dealing with the tax authorities, must act in good faith and exercise care in relation to facts and information presented on behalf of the client or employer. It will

normally be assumed that facts and information on which business tax computations are based were provided by the client or employer as the taxpayer, and the latter bears ultimate responsibility for the accuracy of the facts, information and tax computations. The member shall avoid assuming responsibility for the accuracy of facts, etc. outside his or her knowledge.

'When a member learns of a material error or omission in a tax return of a prior year, or of a failure to file a required tax return, the member has a responsibility to advise promptly the client or employer of the error or omission and recommend that disclosure be made to HMRC. If the client or employer, after having had a reasonable time to reflect, does not correct the error, the member shall inform the client or employer in writing that it is not possible for the member to act for them in connection with that return or other related information submitted to the authorities.'

dealing with professional ethics problems

Dealing with professional ethics can be a difficult and complex area, and we have only outlined some main points. If you find yourself in a position where you are uncertain how you should proceed because of an ethical problem then you should first approach your supervisor or manager. If you are still unable to resolve the problem then further professional or legal advice may need to be obtained.

tax records

It is also important to know what records will need to be kept regarding the client's income and tax affairs, and to ensure that such records are kept secure. The records must be sufficient to substantiate the information provided to HM Revenue & Customs. This would include documentation such as invoices, receipts, and working papers.

These records must be kept as follows:

- **companies** must keep records relating to the information in their tax returns until at least six years after the end of the accounting period. For example, records relating to the Chargeable Accounting Period (CAP) from 1/4/2023 until 31/3/2024 must be kept until 31/3/2030

- **individuals** in business (sole traders and partners) must keep records for approximately five years plus ten months from the end of the tax year to which they relate. For example, documents relating to 2023/24 must be retained until 31 January 2030

For both types of organisation this date for record keeping is five years after the latest filing date for the return (assuming the Income Tax return is submitted online). If there is a formal HM Revenue & Customs enquiry into a taxpayer's affairs then the records need to be kept at least until the end of the enquiry.

There can be a penalty for not keeping the required records of up to £3,000 for each tax year (for individuals) or £3,000 per accounting period (for companies).

compliance checks

HMRC can carry out 'compliance checks' relating to a range of taxes including Corporation Tax, Income Tax and Capital Gains Tax to ensure that the correct amount of tax is paid and that proper records are kept. HMRC has powers to:

- visit businesses to inspect premises, assets and records
- ask taxpayers and third parties (for example, tax practitioners) for more information and documents

In most situations at least seven days prior notice would be given of a visit. HMRC is required by law to 'act reasonably' with regard to compliance checks.

- The taxes that UK businesses are subject to will depend on the type of organisation.

- The profits and gains of limited companies are subject to Corporation Tax, while sole traders and partners' trading profits are subject to Income Tax, along with any other personal income. The self-employed are also subject to Capital Gains Tax on the disposal of certain business assets. National Insurance contributions are applied to the self-employed and partners on their profits.

- Income Tax and Corporation Tax are administered by HM Revenue & Customs, which collects tax and National Insurance Contributions. It is also responsible for publishing documents and forms to gather information about how much tax is owed and is governed by statute law and case law.

- Under both Corporation Tax and Income Tax, the assessable amount is divided into categories so that appropriate rules can be applied to calculate the amount of each different form of income.

- Corporation Tax rates relate to financial years that run from 1 April. The tax is calculated separately for each Chargeable Accounting Period (CAP) that is linked to the period for which the accounts are produced.

- The Company Tax Return (CT600) is based on the CAP. Corporation Tax is payable within nine months and one day after the end of the CAP. Large companies must also make instalment payments.

- Income Tax, which applies to individuals (sole traders and partners), is calculated separately for each tax year (6 April to the following 5 April). An Income Tax computation is used to calculate the tax by totalling the income from various sources, and subtracting the personal allowance. Each tax year has a separate tax return, which is used to collect information about the income and tax of individuals. Income Tax must be paid to HM Revenue & Customs by the 31 January following the end of the tax year. For some taxpayers there is also a requirement to make payments on account before this date.

- National Insurance is applied to the self-employed and partners in respect of their profits. They must pay a flat rate (Class 2), plus an amount calculated as percentages of their profits (Class 4).

- Tax practitioners have responsibilities to their clients (including confidentiality) and to HM Revenue & Customs. They must also ensure that all necessary records are kept for the required period of time.

limited company	a limited company is a separate legal entity from its owners (the shareholders). Its profits are subject to Corporation Tax
sole trader	an individual who is self-employed on his or her own. There is no legal distinction between the business entity and the individual, and the sole trader is subject to Income Tax on the profits of the business
partnership	an organisation made up of several individuals who share the responsibilities and profits of the partnership. Since there is no legal separation between the partnership and the individuals who are partners, they are individually subject to Income Tax on their share of the profits. Effectively, a partnership is a collection of sole traders
Corporation Tax	a tax that applies to the trading and other profits of limited companies, including any chargeable gains
Income Tax	the tax that individuals (including sole traders and partners) pay on their income, including business profits
Capital Gains Tax	the tax that applies to certain disposals that individuals make on business and private assets
National Insurance	effectively a tax that is applied to the self-employed and partners
statute law	legislation that is passed by Parliament – for example, the annual Finance Act
case law	the result of decisions taken in court cases that have an impact on the interpretation of law
financial year (Corporation Tax)	Each financial year runs from 1 April to 31 March. Corporation Tax rates are based on financial years
tax year (Income Tax)	each tax year runs from 6 April to the following 5 April. Tax years are also known as fiscal years
company tax return	this document (the CT600) is filed online for each Chargeable Accounting Period, normally the period for which the company prepares accounts

tax return (individuals)	the self-assessment tax return is issued for each tax year to certain taxpayers and relates to Income Tax and Capital Gains Tax.
tax planning	carrying out financial planning in the most tax-efficient way in order to minimise tax
tax avoidance	minimising tax by legal means (unless avoidance is 'abusive')
tax evasion	illegally relying on concealment, pretence, non-disclosure or misrepresentation to pay less tax

Activities

1.1   The following statements are made by a trainee in the Tax Department of Jenner & Co.

Indicate whether each statement is true or false.

		True	False
(a)	One of the reasons that income is divided into categories is so that the correct rules can be applied to each type of income.		
(b)	The only law that is relevant to tax matters is the current Finance Act.		
(c)	Companies must complete a separate CT600 tax return for every financial year in which they operate.		
(d)	A Corporation Tax Computation is the name given to the calculation of Corporation Tax, based on the taxable total profits chargeable to Corporation Tax for the Chargeable Accounting Period.		
(e)	A sole trader with profits assessable in 2023/24 of £21,570, and no other taxable income, would pay Income Tax of £1,800.		
(f)	It is the job of a tax practitioner to ensure that his client pays the least amount of tax. This may involve bending the rules, or omitting certain items from a tax computation.		
(g)	Most self-employed people pay tax under PAYE and so don't have to worry about completing tax returns.		

1.2 DonCom plc has the following assessable income agreed for the Chargeable Accounting Period from 1/4/2023 to 31/3/2024:

Trading Profits	£1,300,000
Chargeable Gains	£500,000
Profits from renting property	£100,000

Required:

(a) Assuming a Corporation Tax rate of 25%, use a Corporation Tax computation to calculate the tax liability for DonCom plc.

(b) State the filing date of the CT600 form, and the date by which the final Corporation Tax payment must be made.

1.3 Parmajit is trading in partnership. Her share of the partnership profits for the accounting period 1/4/2023 to 31/3/2024 was £16,000. In addition she had other general taxable income in the tax year 2023/24 of £2,000. She uses paper-based tax returns.

Required:

(a) Assuming that Parmajit is entitled to a personal allowance of £12,570 for the tax year, and pays Income Tax at 20% for that year, calculate her Income Tax liability.

(b) State the date that her tax return must be submitted if HM Revenue & Customs were to calculate her tax, and the date by which the balance of Income Tax must be paid for the tax year.

1.4 John is self-employed, and has assessable trading profits for the tax year 2023/24 of £25,000.

Required:

Calculate the National Insurance Contribution liability under each class for John. State how payment would be made.

1.5 You are a trainee employed by Osborne Accounting Practice, working in its Tax Department. The practice uses online return submission for Income Tax. You are currently scheduling work related to two clients as follows:

The Walvern Water Company Limited produces annual accounts to 31 July. The accounts for the year ended 31/7/2023 have been completed and are awaiting the necessary tax work.

Wally Weaver is a sole trader who has been trading for many years. The practice has produced accounts for him for the year ended 31/3/2024.

Required:

- State the type of tax return that will need to be completed for each of the clients.

- Explain how each tax return is related to the client's accounting period, and state the latest submission dates for the returns.

- State in each case the final date for the payment of outstanding tax after any instalments or payments on account have been made.

1.6 **(1)** Which of the following statements is correct?

(a)	Every self-employed taxpayer must pay Class 2 NIC, irrespective of the level of profits.
(b)	Self-employed taxpayers pay either Class 2 or Class 4, but not both.
(c)	Class 4 NIC is based on the amount of money taken out of the business by the taxpayer.
(d)	An individual failing to keep appropriate records for the correct length of time is subject to a penalty of up to £3,000 for each tax year.

(2) A taxpayer has self-employed income of £70,000 for 2023/24.

The amount chargeable to NIC at 2% would be   £ [ ]

(3) A taxpayer has self-employed income of £35,000 for 2023/24.

The amount of total Class 4 NIC payable would be   £ [ ]

1.7   John was an employee for many years, paying Income Tax through PAYE. During the tax year 2022/23 he left his job and became self-employed. The Income Tax liability and Class 4 NIC have been accurately calculated for each of the tax years 2022/23 and 2023/24 as follows:

2022/23   £8,500 (including £2,300 paid via PAYE)

2023/24   £11,000 (none paid via PAYE)

Based on the above figures, complete the following table by inserting the amounts that John was due to pay relating to the tax years 2022/23 to 2024/25 on the dates shown. Insert zeros in any cells that do not apply.

Payment date	31 Jan 2023 £	31 July 2023 £	31 Jan 2024 £	31 July 2024 £	31 Jan 2025 £	31 July 2025 £
Tax year 2022/23						
Tax year 2023/24						
Tax year 2024/25						
Totals due						

2 Corporation Tax – trading profits

this chapter covers...

In this chapter we provide a brief review of the Corporation Tax computation, and examine the step by step procedures for compiling the computation, before concentrating on the calculation of adjusted trading profits.

We examine in detail how to adjust the data provided in an income statement so that it is valid for tax purposes. This involves adjusting income and expenditure. We will note the main types of expenditure that cannot be set against trading income, as well as specific examples of expenditure that is allowable.

There will be opportunities to practise adjusting accounts that have been prepared for internal purposes, as well as using published accounts.

We will then see how to deal with the situation when accounts have been prepared for a long period and need to be split into two Chargeable Accounting Periods.

Finally, we will learn the rather complex rules about the options that are available to companies to offset any trade losses that they incur.

THE CORPORATION TAX COMPUTATION

We saw in the last chapter that the Corporation Tax computation comprises a summary of profits from various sources that are chargeable to Corporation Tax. The computation then goes on to calculate the amount of Corporation Tax that is payable. A simple version of this computation is repeated here:

	Trading income	X
+	Profits from Investments	X
+	Chargeable Gains	X
=	Taxable Total Profits (TTP)	X
	Corporation Tax on taxable total profits	X

Note that 'taxable total profits' were previously known as 'profits chargeable to Corporation Tax' (PCTCT).

You will notice that 'Trading Income' is listed as the first item in the computation, and is often the most important one. We will be looking in detail in this chapter at why and how the trading profits from the financial accounts are adjusted for tax purposes.

Before we do that, we will examine briefly the main steps that need to be undertaken to complete the full Corporation Tax computation. We can then refer to this procedure as we look at the components in detail over the next chapters. The following diagram shows in summary how it all fits together.

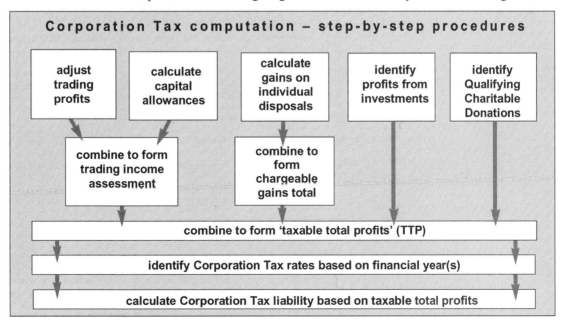

In this chapter we are going to learn how to adjust the trading profit (the top left-hand box in the diagram). We will also see how trade losses can be set against profits to reduce total taxable profits.

In Chapter 3 we will see how to calculate capital allowances so that we can incorporate the result into the trading income assessment.

In Chapter 4 we will examine chargeable gains and then we will see how it all fits together.

In Chapter 5 we will explain how to calculate the Corporation Tax liability.

ADJUSTMENT OF PROFITS

The starting point for the calculation of trading profits is the statement of profit or loss (income statement) that has been prepared by the company. Whether you are asked to work from a set of accounts prepared for internal use, or in published format, the process is the same.

The 'basis of assessment' for trading profits is the **tax-adjusted trading profits** of the **Chargeable Accounting Period**, prepared on an accruals basis. In this section of the book we will start by using accounts that have been prepared for the Chargeable Accounting Period (ie no more than 12 months). We will see later how we deal with accounts that have been prepared for a longer period. Since the financial accounts that will be our starting point will always have been prepared on an accruals basis, that aspect should not cause us any problems.

The reason that accounts need to be adjusted for tax purposes is not because they are wrong, but because Corporation Tax does not use exactly the same rules as financial accounting. We need to arrive at a profit figure that is based on the tax rules! For example, there are some costs that although quite legitimate from an accounting point of view are not allowable as a deduction in arriving at the profit figure for tax purposes.

The object of adjusting the financial accounts is to make sure that:

- the only **income** that is credited is **trading income**
- the only **expenditure** that is deducted is **allowable trading expenditure**

When we adjust profits, we will start with the profit from the financial accounts, and

- deduct any income that is not trading income, and
- add back any expenditure that has already been deducted but is not allowable

This approach is much more convenient than re-writing the whole profit and loss account based on tax rules. It is quite logical, because it effectively cancels out income and expenditure that is not relevant for tax purposes.

example – adjusting the profits

Suppose that we wish to adjust a set of financial accounts (shown here in summary form):

	£000
Sales	500
less cost of sales	200
Gross trading profit	300
Non-trading income	150
	450
less expenditure	120
Net profit	330

Analysis of the accounts has shown that the cost of sales is entirely allowable, but £40,000 of the £120,000 expenditure is not allowable for tax purposes.

To adjust the profits we would carry out the following computation:

	£000
Net profit per accounts	330
less non-trading income	(150)
Add expenditure that is not allowable	40
Adjusted trading profit	220

This provides us with the same answer that we could get by writing out the accounts in full, using only the trading income and allowable expenditure. If we did that it would look as follows. This is shown just for comparison – we won't actually need to rewrite the accounts in this way.

	£000
Sales	500
less allowable cost of sales	200
Gross trading profit	300
less allowable expenditure	80
Net profit	220

We will now look in more detail at adjustments for income, followed by expenditure.

adjusting income

Provided the 'sales', 'turnover' or 'revenue' figure relates entirely to trading, this figure will not need adjusting. Other income may or may not be taxable, but if it is not trading income, then it will need to be adjusted for in the trading profit calculation.

The following are examples of income that are **not assessable as trading income**, and should therefore be adjusted for by **deducting** from the net profit shown in the financial accounts:

- non-trading interest receivable

- rent receivable (property income)

- gains on the disposal of non-current assets (fixed assets)

- dividends received

All these examples should be adjusted by simply deducting the amount that was credited to the financial accounts. There is no need to worry about exactly how the figure was originally calculated. We will then have arrived at what the profit would have been if these items had not been included originally. Items that originate from the trade (eg discounts received) are taxable as part of trading income, and therefore need no adjustment.

Non-trading interest and **rent received** will reappear in the taxable total profits (TTP) computation as investment income and property income, respectively. Throughout the examples in this book, you can assume that any interest received is non-trading and is therefore dealt with as outlined here, unless stated otherwise.

Gains on the disposal of non-current assets could result in chargeable gains. These gains need to be calculated according to special rules before being incorporated into the taxable total profits as we will see in Chapter 4. **Dividends received** from UK companies are not assessable under Corporation Tax at all (since they have been paid out of another company's taxed income).

adjusting expenditure

We will only need to adjust for any expenditure accounted for in the financial accounts profit if it is **not allowable**. We do this by **adding it back** to the financial accounts profit. Expenditure that is allowable can be left unadjusted in the accounts. Although this may seem obvious, it is easy to get confused.

The general rule for expenditure to be allowable in a trading income computation is that it must be:

- revenue rather than capital in nature, and

- 'wholly and exclusively' for the purpose of the trade

Although we will look at how to deal with various specific types of expenditure shortly, these rules are fundamental, and should always be used to guide you in the absence of more precise information. This part of the unit will require a good deal of study, since it is quite complex, and the rules and examples that follow will need to be remembered. The best way to approach this is to continually revise the topic and practise lots of examples.

expenditure that is not allowable

The following are examples of expenditure that is not allowable, and therefore requires adjustment. Some clearly follow the rules outlined above, while others may have arisen from specific regulations, or court cases forming precedents (case law).

■ **any capital expenditure**

This follows the normal financial accounting use of the term, to mean expenditure on assets that will have a value to the business over several accounting periods. Capital expenditure includes expenditure to improve non-current assets, and installation costs and legal expenses in connection with acquiring non-current assets. It also includes repairs to a newly acquired non-current asset that are necessary to bring it into working condition.

■ **depreciation of non-current assets**

This is because capital allowances are allowable instead, as HM Revenue & Customs' alternative to depreciation, as we will see in the next chapter. Even where there are no capital allowances available, depreciation is still not allowed. Other items which are similar to depreciation (eg amortisation of certain assets, and losses on disposal of non-current assets) are also not allowable.

■ **part of lease rental payments for high emission cars**

When a car with an emission level of more than 50 g/km of CO_2 is leased for over 45 days through an operating lease, 15% of the lease rental payment is disallowed, leaving an allowable expenditure of 85% of the payment. If the car has emission levels lower than this then all of the lease rental payment is allowable.

■ **entertaining expenditure**

This relates to business entertaining of customers or suppliers. Entertaining of the businesses' own staff is, however, allowable (see page 35).

■ **gifts to customers**

Virtually all gifts made to customers are not allowable. There is an exception for some low-value items, as we will see shortly.

■ **increases in general bad debt provisions**

Any such increase (that is debited to the income statement) must be added back in the computation, and decreases in general provisions adjusted for by deducting from profits. A general provision could be based on a lump sum, or a percentage of total trade receivables (debtors). Increases in specific provisions and the actual write-off of bad debts are, however, allowable. Where accounts have been prepared using 'impairment' as a means of calculating the bad debt provision, the provision will be treated in the same way as a specific bad debt provision. This applies as long as objective evidence was used to calculate the amount of impairment. This situation could arise if, for example, the accounts are prepared under International Accounting Standards. See also the additional note on page 36.

■ **charitable payments**

These items can be deducted from the total profits of the company in the taxable total profits (TTP) calculation as 'Qualifying Charitable Donations' (QCDs). Where this occurs the expenditure cannot also be deducted in the calculation of trading profits. We will look a little more closely at these payments in Chapter 5.

■ **fines for law breaking**

Fines imposed on the company itself for lawbreaking (eg for breaches of health & safety legislation) are not allowable, nor are the associated legal costs. The costs of tax appeals are also not allowable. Fines for minor motoring offences incurred by employees whilst on business are allowable, but not if the employee is a Director of the company.

■ **certain legal expenses**

Legal expenses incurred on forming a company or acquiring new leases (both long and short leases).

■ **illegal payments**

For example bribes, or payments made in response to threats.

■ **donations to political parties**

These are not for the purpose of 'the trade' and so are not allowable.

■ **writing off non-trade loans**

For example, loans to employees or directors (unless they were incurred in the normal course of trade).

■ **dividends payable**

The payment of dividends is not an allowable expense. However, if these occur in the accounts after the net profit that we have used as the starting point for our calculation, there will be no need for an adjustment.

■ **Corporation Tax**

Logically, the tax payment itself is not tax deductible!

expenditure that is allowable

As already stated, revenue expenditure that is 'wholly and exclusively' for the purpose of the trade is allowable. We will now list some illustrative examples, a few of which were referred to above.

▪ normal **cost of sales**

▪ normal **business expenditure**, for example:
  – distribution costs
  – administration
  – salaries and wages, and employers' NIC
  – rent, rates and insurance
  – repairs
  – advertising
  – business travel and subsistence
  – accountancy services
  – research & development expenditure

▪ **specifically allowable expenditure:**
  – operating lease rental payments for cars with emission levels of 50 g/km or less
  – legal expenses on renewing (but not acquiring) a short (ie 50 years or shorter) lease
  – interest payable on trade loans
  – staff entertaining (eg staff Christmas parties)
  – trade bad debts written off (note, however, that writing off of a loan to an employee is not allowable, since it is not a trade item)
  – increases in specific provisions for trade bad debts and impairment provisions based on objective evidence (see note below). Specific provisions are those based on named debtors
  – gifts to customers that contain a conspicuous advertisement, costing up to £50 per recipient per year; this, however, does not apply to food, drink, tobacco or gift vouchers, gifts of which can never be allowable – allowable examples would include calendars and diaries
  – gifts of trading stock to educational establishments, charities or registered amateur sports clubs
  – employees' parking fines incurred while on business, but not those of directors

■   **capital allowances**

We will see how to calculate capital allowances in the next chapter. In the exercises in this chapter we will use capital allowance figures that have already been calculated. Because capital allowances will not be recorded in the financial accounts, they will be deducted as a separate item in the adjustment to the accounts.

note regarding repairs – capital or revenue?

We have seen that repairs to bring a newly acquired non-current asset up to operating standard are capital expenditure, and therefore not allowable, and that other repairs are generally allowable. Allowable repairs can include replacement of parts of a non-current asset (for example, replacing a car gearbox), but not replacing the whole asset itself (for example, replacing the car), which would be capital expenditure.

While the general rule is that improvement to a non-current asset is considered capital expenditure and therefore not allowable, there is an exception where a replacement part is better than the original part due to changing technology. This could be, for example, where the replacement part must meet current standards, or where it is in line with current industry norms. In these situations, the replacement part is considered to be an allowable revenue cost. An example of this is the replacement of original single-glazed windows with modern double-glazed ones, which has been agreed to be allowable revenue expenditure. Here the windows themselves are not considered to be the non-current assets, but they are simply part of the whole building which forms the asset.

note regarding trade bad debts and provisions

Whereas a sum written off a trade debt or an increase in a specific provision is allowable, any recovery of amounts previously written off and any decrease in specific provisions is taxable, and no adjustment is needed. This can be a confusing area. The following table summarises the position:

Expenditure	Treatment	Action
Trade Bad Debts Written Off	Allowable	No adjustment
Increases in Specific Bad Debt Provisions	Allowable	No adjustment
Increases in General Bad Debt Provisions	Not allowable	Add back
Income	**Treatment**	**Action**
Trade Bad Debts Recovered	Taxable	No adjustment
Decreases in Specific Bad Debt Provisions	Taxable	No adjustment
Decreases in General Bad Debt Provisions	Not taxable	Deduct

Case Study

TRADING ALOUD LIMITED: ADJUSTING THE PROFIT

Trading Aloud Limited is a company that specialises in selling acoustic equipment. The unadjusted income statement for the year ended 31/3/2024 is as follows:

	Notes	£	£
Sales			900,000
less cost of sales			530,000
Gross profit			370,000
Rental income			120,000
Dividends received			140,000
less expenses:			630,000
Salaries and wages	(1)	95,400	
Depreciation		51,000	
Directors' fees		45,000	
Administration expenses		17,600	
Advertising	(2)	12,600	
Travel and entertaining	(3)	19,500	
Bad debts and provisions	(4)	21,650	
			262,750
Net Profit			367,250

Notes:

(1) Salaries and wages includes £4,350 employers' NIC.

(2) Advertising includes:

    (a) gifts of food hampers to 70 customers £3,250

    (b) gifts of 100 mouse-mats with company logos £500

(3) Travel and entertaining is made up as follows:

	£
Employees' travel expenses	7,400
Employees' subsistence allowances	5,450
Entertaining customers	6,650
	19,500

(4) Bad debts and provisions is made up of:

	£
Trade bad debts written off	13,400
Increase in general bad debt provision	5,000
Increase in specific bad debt provision	3,250
	21,650

Capital allowances for the period have been calculated at £15,000.

required

Adjust the net profit shown to arrive at the trading income assessment for Corporation Tax purposes.

solution

The computation is shown here with notes that explain the rationale behind each adjustment and allowed item. Items that are to be deducted are shown in the left-hand column, and those to be added kept in the main (right-hand) column for clarity.

		£
Net Profit per accounts		367,250
Add Back:		
Expenditure that is shown in the accounts but is not allowable		
Depreciation		51,000
Food Hampers		3,250
Entertaining Customers		6,650
Increase in General Bad Debt Provision		5,000
		433,150
Deduct:		
Income not taxable as trading income	£	
Rental Income	120,000	
Dividends Received	140,000	
Capital Allowances	15,000	
		(275,000)
Trading Income Assessment		158,150

Notes:

- The sales and cost of sales appear to be normal trading items.

- The rental income will be brought into the main Corporation Tax computation as property income.

- The dividends received are not subject to Corporation Tax.

- Salaries and Wages (including employers' NIC) are allowable.

- Depreciation is never allowable.

- Directors' fees are treated in the same way as other staff salaries.

- Administration expenses appear to be wholly and exclusively for the trade.

- The advertising costs are allowable, including the mouse-mats that fall under the provision regarding items under £50 per person. The hampers cannot be covered by this rule as they contain food.

- Employees' travel and subsistence costs are allowable, but entertaining customers is never allowable.

- Changes in general provisions for bad debts must always be adjusted for, but specific provision increases and bad debts written off are allowable.

- The capital allowance figure is shown here as a final deduction in arriving at the assessable trading income.

working from published accounts

The principle of adjusting profits for tax purposes is the same when using a published version of financial accounts. The only issue that requires extra care is the choice of profit figure as a starting point from the range of figures available. It makes sense to use the profit figure that will require the least number of adjustments. The best profit figure to use will therefore be profit before tax so that this item will not need further adjustment. We will now use a Case Study to illustrate this procedure. Since you will probably be familiar with the International Accounting Standards (IAS) format, we will use it here.

Case Study

FORMAT COMPANY LIMITED: ADJUSTING PUBLISHED ACCOUNTS

The published accounts of Format Company Limited under IAS for the year ended 31 March 2024 are shown below, together with notes that provide some analysis of the summarised data.

Capital allowances have already been calculated, and amount to £86,400.

	£000
Revenue	963
Cost of Sales	(541)
Gross Profit	422
Other Income	390
Distribution Costs	(56)
Administrative Expenses	(123)
Finance Costs	(24)
Profit before Tax	609
Tax	(150)
Profit for the Year	459

Notes:

- Cost of Sales includes depreciation of £140,000
- Administrative Expenses include the following:
  - Increase in Bad Debt Provision due to impairment
    calculation based on objective evidence   £7,700
  - Entertaining Customers   £9,600
- Other Income consists of:
  - Rental Income   £220,000
  - Interest Received from Investments   £60,000

– Profit on Sale of Non-current Assets	£95,000
– Dividends Received	£15,000

- Finance Costs relates to bank overdraft interest.

required

Calculate the trading income as adjusted for tax purposes.

solution

We will start our computation with the 'Profit before Tax' since the item that follows that figure is not allowable, whereas the items that precede it could be a mixture of allowable and non-allowable.

	£	£
Profit before Tax		609,000
Add Back:		
Expenditure that is shown in the accounts but is not allowable:		
Depreciation		140,000
Entertaining Customers		9,600
		758,600
Deduct:		
Income that is not taxable as trading income:		
Rental Income	220,000	
Interest Received from Investments	60,000	
Profit on Sale of Non-current Assets	95,000	
Dividends Received	15,000	
Capital Allowances	86,400	(476,400)
Trading Income Assessment		282,200

DEALING WITH ACCOUNTS FOR LONG PERIODS

In Chapter 1 we saw that a **Chargeable Accounting Period** (CAP – the period that we must use for Corporation Tax purposes) is the same as the period that the accounts have been prepared for, but only if that period is for 12 months or less. Where the company produces its financial accounts for a period exceeding 12 months, this will be divided into two CAPs (and require two Corporation Tax computations):

- one CAP for the first 12 months of the financial accounting period and

- one CAP for the balance of the financial accounting period

For example, if a company produces financial accounts for the 18 month period 1/7/2022 to 31/12/2023, there will be two CAPs:

- a 12 month CAP: 1/7/2022 to 30/6/2023, and

- a 6 month CAP: 1/7/2023 to 31/12/2023

The mechanism for dealing with the two Corporation Tax computations for these periods is:

- the financial accounts for the long period are adjusted in one operation, with the exception of the capital allowances deduction

- the adjusted profits (before the deduction of any capital allowance) are then time-apportioned into the two CAPs

- capital allowances are calculated separately for each CAP (as we will see in the next chapter)

- each CAP's adjusted trading profit is then finalised by deducting the capital allowances that have been calculated for the specific period

We will now use a Case Study to illustrate this principle.

Case Study

THYME LIMITED: ACCOUNTS FOR A LONG PERIOD

Thyme Limited is changing its accounting dates, and to accommodate this has produced one long set of financial accounts, from 1/10/2022 to 31/3/2024.

Capital allowances have already been calculated for each of the two CAPs as follows:

CAP 1/10/2022 to 30/9/2023   £15,000

CAP 1/10/2023 to 31/3/2024   £6,000

The financial accounts for the 18 months to 31/3/2024 are shown on the next page.

The following information is also provided:

- salaries and wages relate to the two directors, who are the only employees

- depreciation etc is made up as follows:
  - Depreciation   £35,000
  - Loss on sale of motors   £9,500
  - Profit on sale of building   (£33,500)

- selling expenses include:
  - Entertaining customers   £4,700
  - Gifts of wine to customers   £1,900
  - Gifts of calendars to customers   £500
    (£10 each, with company advert)

- general expenses include accountancy fees of £2,800
- bad debts are made up of:

  – Increase in specific provision   £8,000

  – Bad debts written off   £23,600

  – Bad debts recovered   (£12,200)

Thyme Limited
Financial accounts for the 18 months to 31/3/2024

	£	£
Sales		237,000
less cost of sales		103,000
Gross profit		134,000
less expenses:		
Salaries and wages	43,500	
Rent, rates, and insurance	8,700	
Depreciation etc	11,000	
Selling expenses	15,780	
General expenses	15,630	
Bad Debts	19,400	
		114,010
Net Profit		19,990

required

1 Adjust the financial accounts for the 18-month period, before deduction of capital allowances.

2 Time-apportion the adjusted profit figure into CAPs.

3 Calculate the trading income assessment for each CAP.

solution

1

	£	£
Net Profit for 18-month period per accounts		19,990
Add back non-allowable expenditure:		
Depreciation		35,000
Loss on sale of motors		9,500
Entertaining customers		4,700
Gifts of wine		1,900
		71,090
Deduct income that is not taxable as trading income		
Profit on sale of building	33,500	
		(33,500)
Adjusted profit before capital allowances		37,590

Notes:

- The profit on the sale of the building is not taxable as trading income, and is therefore deducted. An alternative approach would be to add back the net £11,000 that relates to the three items under the heading of 'depreciation'.

- The calendars are allowable under the gift rules.

- All the items under the bad debts heading are allowable/taxable, and therefore do not require adjustment.

2 The adjusted profit for the 18-month period is time-apportioned as follows:

CAP 1/10/2022 to 30/9/2023   £37,590 × 12/18   =   £25,060

CAP 1/10/2023 to 31/3/2024   £37,590 × 6/18   =   £12,530

3 Capital allowances are then deducted from the adjusted profit for each CAP:

	1/10/22 – 30/9/23	1/10/23 – 31/3/24
	£	£
Adjusted profit	25,060	12,530
Capital allowances	15,000	6,000
Trading Income	10,060	6,530

DEALING WITH TRADE LOSSES

If, once profits have been tax-adjusted and any capital allowances deducted, the result is a minus figure, a 'trading loss' will have arisen. This will have two implications:

- the **trading income assessment** for the Chargeable Accounting Period will be zero (not the negative profit figure)
- the amount of the **negative profit figure** will form the **trading loss**, and the company can choose how to deal with it

How does one deal with this situation? The options are as follows:

1   A trading loss can be carried forward to set against the **total profits** (TTP before Qualifying Charitable Donation (QCD) deduction) of future CAPs, within certain limits. The limits are outside the scope of your studies. The company may choose which future CAP(s) to offset the loss against.

2   The trading loss can be used to reduce (or eliminate) all of the taxable total profits (TTP before QCD deduction) in the same CAP that the loss arose. This set off would be against all taxable investment income and chargeable gains for the period, before deducting QCD payments.

3   Only if option (2) above is chosen can the loss then be carried back against the taxable total profits (TTP before QCD deduction) of the CAP in the 12 months immediately before the one in which the loss occurred. If there were two CAPs partly falling into that 12-month period, then both could be used.

   In this situation, the profits of the CAP that is only partly within the 12-month period would need to be time apportioned. Only the part of the profit falling within the 12-month period can be used against the loss.

The diagram on the next page illustrates these options, using as an example a company making up accounts to the 31 December each year. A loss arises in the year ended 31/12/2023.

We will discuss Qualifying Charitable Donations/QCDs in more detail in Chapter 5.

The time limit for claiming loss relief under options 2 and 3 is 2 years from the end of the CAP in which the loss was incurred.

terminal loss relief

Where a company ceases trading, and it incurs a trading loss in the last 12 months of its business, terminal loss relief can be claimed. This enables the company to set the loss of the last 12 months against taxable total profits (TTP before QCD deduction) for the three years before that period. The loss is set against the later years first. For each year used to offset the loss, the company must have been carrying out the same trade as the one in which the loss was incurred.

Where a CAP falls partly into the three-year period, then its profits must be time-apportioned, as in the carry-back option for normal losses.

The time limit for claiming terminal loss relief is two years from the end of the CAP in which the loss was incurred.

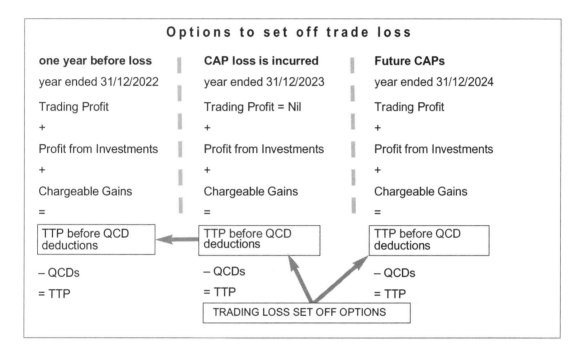

Options to set off trade loss

one year before loss	**CAP loss is incurred**	**Future CAPs**
year ended 31/12/2022	year ended 31/12/2023	year ended 31/12/2024
Trading Profit	Trading Profit = Nil	Trading Profit
+	+	+
Profit from Investments	Profit from Investments	Profit from Investments
+	+	+
Chargeable Gains	Chargeable Gains	Chargeable Gains
=	=	=
TTP before QCD deductions	TTP before QCD deductions	TTP before QCD deductions
– QCDs	– QCDs	– QCDs
= TTP	= TTP	= TTP

TRADING LOSS SET OFF OPTIONS

Where option (2) has been used, or option (2) followed by option (3), and the whole loss has still not been offset, any balance will follow option (1).

We can now revise our diagram (see page 29) illustrating the Corporation Tax Computation procedures to incorporate possible trading loss set off. The dark box is an addition to the diagram.

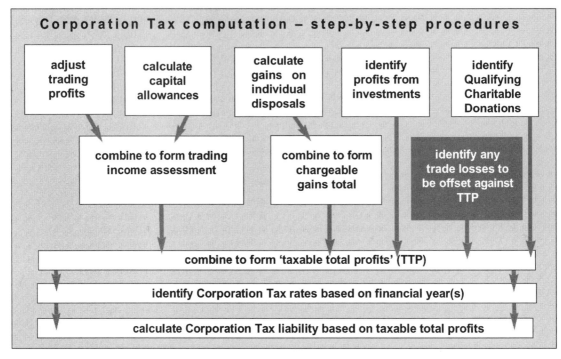

We will now use a Case Study to illustrate these options. We will also return to this topic in later chapters when we have studied the build-up of the taxable total profits (TTP) in more detail.

Case Study

DOWNSEA PANS LIMITED: TRADING LOSS OPTIONS

Downsea Pans Limited has the following tax-adjusted results for the three Chargeable Accounting Periods to 31/12/2024. The company continued to trade.

CAP	year ended 31/12/22	year ended 31/12/23	year ended 31/12/24
	£000	£000	£000
Trading Profit/(Loss)	120	(150)	160
Profits from investments	40	50	55
Chargeable gains	75	15	80

The company did not make any Qualifying Charitable Donations payments.

required

State the options available for offsetting the £150,000 trading loss incurred in the CAP year ended 31/12/2023.

Demonstrate the effects on the relevant taxable total profits (TTP) figures by showing Corporation Tax computation extracts.

solution

We will show the options one by one, but with all the three years' details shown in columnar form for reference.

Option One

The trading loss could be carried forward and set against the TTP of y/e 31/12/2024 (or a later CAP). Since this profit is larger than the loss, the whole loss could be offset in this way. The Corporation Tax computation extract for y/e 31/12/2024 would be affected, and the three years would look as follows:

	y/e 31/12/22	y/e 31/12/23	y/e 31/12/24
	£000	£000	£000
Trading Income	120	0	160
Profits from Investments	40	50	55
Chargeable Gains	75	15	80
less loss relief			(150)
TTP	235	65	145

Option Two

The trading loss could be set against the other profits and chargeable gains of the CAP y/e 31/12/2023 (the CAP in which the loss was incurred). Due to the size of the loss this will not be sufficient to offset the whole loss. The balance of the loss could then be carried back to the CAP y/e 31/12/2022 and set against the TTP in that period as well. This would give the following Corporation Tax computation extracts:

	y/e 31/12/22	y/e 31/12/23	y/e 31/12/24
	£000	£000	£000
Trading Income	120	0	160
Profits from Investments	40	50	55
Chargeable Gains	75	15	80
	235	65	295
less loss relief			
first set off		(65)	
second set off	(85)		
TTP	150	0	295

Note that the loss can only be carried back after the current year set off has been carried out to its full extent.

Option Three

Following the current year set off as in option two, the previous year's TTP need not be utilised. In that case the balance of the loss could be carried forward against

the TTP of y/e 31/12/2024 (or a later CAP). This would give the following figures for the three years.

	y/e 31/12/22	y/e 31/12/23	y/e 31/12/24
	£000	£000	£000
Trading Income	120	0	160
Profits from Investments	40	50	55
Chargeable Gains	75	15	80
	235	65	295
less loss relief (first set off)		(65)	
less loss relief (second set off)			(85)
TTP	235	0	210

The actual choice of option would depend on factors such as cash flow and the tax rates that would apply to the levels of TTP in each year. We will examine this issue in Chapter 5.

Chapter Summary

- The 'taxable total profits' (TTP) include trading income, profits from investments, and chargeable gains. To arrive at the trading income, the profits based on the financial accounts must be adjusted, and capital allowances calculated and deducted from the adjusted profit figure.

- To adjust the profit based on the financial accounts, any income shown in the accounts that is not taxable as trading income is deducted, and any expenditure that is not allowable is added. The capital allowances that will have been calculated separately are then deducted to arrive at the assessable trading income.

- To be allowable, expenditure must be revenue (not capital), and wholly and exclusively for the purpose of the trade. There are also detailed rules about whether certain items of expenditure are allowable.

- Where the financial accounts are prepared for a period exceeding twelve months, the period will form two Chargeable Accounting Periods. One CAP will be for the first twelve months, and the other for the balance of the financial accounting period. To deal with this situation, the financial accounts are adjusted as a whole, apart from the capital allowances. The adjusted profit is then time-apportioned into the two CAPs, and separate capital allowance figures deducted from each to form two trading income assessments.

- Where the adjusted trading profits (after capital allowances) result in a negative figure, the trading income assessment is zero, and a trading loss is formed that can be relieved in several ways. It may be carried forward and set off against the taxable total profits before Qualifying Charitable Donation (QCD) deductions of future CAPs. It may alternatively be set

against the taxable total profits (TTP before any QCD deductions) of the CAP in which the loss was incurred. Where this happens and not all the loss is used up, the balance can be carried back against the taxable total profits (TTP before any QCD deductions) arising in the preceding twelve months.

▪ Where a trading loss is incurred in the final 12 months before a company ceases trading, terminal loss relief can be claimed, and the loss set against the three years preceding the year of the loss (latest first).

Key Terms

taxable total profits (TTP) — the figure used as the basis for calculation of Corporation Tax for a limited company. It includes trading profits, profits from investments, and chargeable gains. It is calculated for each Chargeable Accounting Period (CAP) that the company operates in

Chargeable Accounting Period (CAP)

the period for which the taxable total profit (TTP) must be calculated. It is the same as the period for which the company produces financial accounts, unless that period is for more than twelve months. In that case the financial accounting period is divided into two CAPs

adjusted trading profits — the trading profits that have been adjusted for tax purposes by excluding income not taxable as trading income, and non-allowable expenditure

trading income assessment — the taxable trading profits for the CAP. It is made up of adjusted trading profits, after deducting any capital allowances

trading loss — this occurs when the adjusted trading profits after deducting capital allowances produces a negative figure. The negative figure is the trading loss, whilst the trading income assessment is zero

loss relief — the offsetting of the trading loss against taxable total profits (TTP)

Activities

2.1   The numbered items listed below appear in an income statement (before the net profit figure).

If you are adjusting the trading profit for tax purposes, state whether each item should be:

- added to the net profit
- deducted from the net profit
- ignored for adjustment purposes

1   accountancy fees payable

2   amortisation of lease

3   non-trade interest received

4   dividends received

5   employees' travel expenses payable

6   gain on sale of non-current asset

7   decrease in specific provision for bad debts

8   gifts of cigars (with company adverts) to customers, costing £40 per recipient

9   increase in general bad debt provision

10   donation to political party

11   employers' National Insurance contributions

12   Qualifying Charitable Donation

2.2   Ahoy Trading Limited is a company that specialises in selling yachting equipment.

The unadjusted income statement for the accounting year is as follows:

	£
Sales	500,000
less cost of sales	220,000
Gross profit	280,000
Interest received	20,000
Dividends received	70,000
	370,000

less expenses:	£	£
Salaries and wages	99,000	
Depreciation	42,000	
Loss on sale of non-current assets	5,000	
Administration expenses	19,600	
Advertising	18,000	
Interest payable	22,000	
Travel and entertaining	19,100	
Bad debts and provisions	15,000	
		239,700
Net Profit		130,300

Notes:

- Administration includes £350 employees' parking fines incurred while on company business.

- Advertising includes:

  – gifts of chocolates with company logos to 100 top customers £4,900

  – gifts of sailing books with company logos to 200 other customers £5,000

- Travel and entertaining is made up as follows:

	£
– Employees' travel expenses	3,400
– Employees' subsistence allowances	5,600
– Entertaining customers	6,000
– Entertaining staff at Christmas	4,100
	19,100

- Bad debts and provisions is made up of:

	£
– Trade bad debts written off	18,400
– Decrease in general bad debt provision	(5,000)
– Increase in specific bad debt provision	1,600
	15,000

Capital allowances for the period have been calculated at £23,000.

Required:

Adjust the net profit shown to arrive at the trading income assessment for Corporation Tax purposes.

2.3 All I Need Trading Limited has an unadjusted income statement for the accounting year as follows:

	£	£
Sales		770,000
less cost of sales		420,000
Gross profit		350,000
Interest received		40,000
Gains on disposal of non-current assets		50,000
Rental income received		60,000
		500,000
less expenses:		
Discounts allowed	10,000	
Salaries and wages	80,500	
Depreciation	51,000	
Bad debts written off	12,000	
Rates and insurance	12,500	
Postage and stationery	11,050	
Administration expenses	12,600	
Advertising	14,000	
Travel and entertaining	19,750	
		223,400
Net Profit		276,600

Notes:

- Administration includes £2,000 directors' speeding fines incurred while on company business.

- Advertising consists of:
  - gifts of CDs with company logos to 1000 customers £9,000
  - gift vouchers with company logos to 200 other customers £5,000

- Travel and entertaining is made up as follows:

	£
Employees' travel expenses	6,400
Employees' subsistence allowances	5,600
Entertaining customers	4,000
Entertaining staff on company trip to races	3,750
	19,750

Capital allowances for the period have been calculated at £31,500.

Required:

Adjust the net profit shown to arrive at the trading income assessment for Corporation Tax purposes.

2.4 Mint Limited is changing its accounting dates, and to accommodate this has produced a set of financial accounts over an extended period, from 1/12/2022 to 31/3/2024.

Capital allowances have already been calculated for each of the two CAPs as follows:

CAP 1/12/2022 to 30/11/2023   £8,000
CAP 1/12/2023 to 31/3/2024   £2,500

The financial accounts for the 16 months to 31/3/2024 are as follows:

	£	£
Sales		293,000
less cost of sales		155,000
Gross profit		138,000
add:		
Bad debts recovered		3,100
Discounts received		2,000
		143,100
less expenses:		
Salaries and wages	68,500	
Rent, rates, and insurance	9,200	
Depreciation etc	10,000	
General expenses	15,630	
Interest payable	8,300	
Bad debts written off	12,400	
Selling expenses	15,000	
		139,030
Net Profit		4,070

The following information is also provided:

- depreciation etc is made up as follows:

Depreciation	£45,000
Loss on sale of computer	£19,500
Profit on sale of Building	£54,500

- general expenses include debt recovery fees of £800

- selling expenses include:

Entertaining customers	£1,930
Gifts of diaries to customers (£6 each, with company advert)	£600

Required:

- Adjust the financial accounts for the 16-month period, before deduction of capital allowances.

- Time-apportion the adjusted profit figure into CAPs.

- Calculate the trading income assessment for each CAP.

2.5 The published accounts of Doormat Company Limited for the year ended 31 March 2024 are shown below, together with notes that provide some analysis of the summarised data. Capital allowances have already been calculated, and amount to £153,000.

	£000
Revenue	743
Cost of Sales	(302)
Gross Profit	441
Other Income	290
Distribution Costs	(144)
Administrative Expenses	(243)
Finance Costs	(50)
Profit before Tax	294
Tax	(71)
Profit for the Year	223

Notes:

- Cost of Sales includes depreciation of £20,000.

- Administrative Expenses include the following:

Loan to employee written off	£8,000
Increase in Specific Bad Debt Provision	£2,800
Increase In General Bad Debt Provision	£7,700
Entertaining Customers	£9,100

- Other Income consists of:

Rental Income	£200,000
Discounts received from trade suppliers	£12,000
Interest Received from Investments	£30,000
Profit on Sale of Non-current Assets	£33,000
Dividends Received	£15,000

- Finance Costs relates to bank overdraft interest.

Required:

- Calculate the trading income assessable figure as adjusted for tax purposes, and the amount of any trading loss.

- State how the trading loss could be relieved without carrying it forward to future periods.

2.6   State whether the following statements are true or false:

		True	False
(a)	Expenditure on purchasing a secondhand van is an example of revenue expenditure		
(b)	Expenditure on purchasing a new van is an example of capital expenditure		
(c)	If a company wishes to carry a loss forward, then it can only set it off against trading profits from the same trade		
(d)	A company can opt to set a trade loss against the taxable total profits (TTP) of the year before the loss whether or not it has first set the loss against the taxable total profits (TTP) relating to the year of the loss		

3 Corporation Tax – capital allowances

this chapter covers...

In this chapter we firstly examine in detail the capital allowances that are available on 'plant and machinery' for companies. These allowances are used instead of depreciation on certain non-current assets for Corporation Tax purposes.

We will examine what is classed as 'plant and machinery' for capital allowances purposes, and then go on to see what type of allowances are available.

We will learn about 'Full Expensing' and about the 'Annual Investment Allowance' and then examine the other capital allowances that can be claimed. We will see how capital allowance computations involve pooling certain assets together while keeping others separate.

The next section is devoted to calculating capital allowances for short Chargeable Accounting Periods, and how the length of period affects some (but not all) allowances.

In the final section we will examine the capital allowances that are available for structures and buildings.

INTRODUCTION TO CAPITAL ALLOWANCES

As we saw in the last chapter, depreciation of non-current (fixed) assets is not an allowable expense for Corporation Tax purposes, but **capital allowances** are often provided instead.

A **capital allowance** reduces the taxable profit for a Chargeable Accounting Period. It results from the acquisition and use of certain non-current assets.

Capital allowances are not, however, automatically available for any non-current asset owned and depreciated by a company. Although many categories of non-current asset do attract capital allowances, there are some that do not. The company's own depreciation policy is also irrelevant when calculating the amount of capital allowance that can be claimed – the same HM Revenue & Customs rules apply for all companies.

To be eligible for capital allowances, the expenditure on the non-current assets must firstly be defined as **capital expenditure**, rather than revenue. Here the definition of capital is generally the same as in financial accounting – expenditure on assets that will benefit the business over several accounting periods.

Secondly, the expenditure must be on assets that attract specific capital allowances. There are several categories of capital allowances, but here we will be examining the main rules relating to **Plant and Machinery**. Later in the chapter we will examine the capital allowances for **Structures and Buildings.**

Capital allowances are claimable for each Chargeable Accounting Period (CAP) separately, based on expenditure incurred in that period and any balances of expenditure brought forward. We will see exactly how this works shortly.

For all expenditure on non-current assets that attract plant and machinery capital allowances, it does not matter how the funding is obtained, whether from:

- cash reserves and money in the bank
- a loan
- hire purchase
- finance leases of at least five years

In all these cases capital allowances are available on the full capital cost as soon as the expenditure is incurred – not when all payments have finally been made. Any interest on loans or hire purchase agreements etc are not capital expenditure, but form allowable revenue expenditure.

If, however, an asset is leased on an **operating lease** then no capital allowances are available as the expenditure is treated as **revenue** as we saw in Chapter 2.

WHAT IS 'PLANT AND MACHINERY'?

Plant and machinery capital allowances form a major area of study in this Unit, and a large number of assets come under this category. As we will see, 'plant and machinery' covers not only items that most of us would expect to be classified in this way, but also a number of unexpected types of asset.

The exact definition of 'plant and machinery' has been subject to debate and modification through statute and case law over the years. One idea that may be useful as a starting point is that plant and machinery covers 'apparatus with which' the business operates, rather than assets 'in which' the business operates. This excludes assets which are simply part of 'the setting' of the business (eg buildings) from being plant and machinery. Examples of plant and machinery that we will deal with are listed below. Both new and second-hand items qualify.

- **plant or machinery** in the normal use of the phrase. This includes moveable and fixed items and their installation costs, and ranges from factory conveyor equipment to cement mixers
- **vans, lorries, and other commercial vehicles**. This category also includes tractors, trailers and other specialist vehicles
- **cars** owned by a limited company and used by the employees (including for private use) are included as plant and machinery
- **furniture, carpets and other moveable items**. Equipment such as specialist lighting used for shop displays or to create atmosphere have been classed as plant and machinery
- **computers and other electronic equipment**. This includes 'information and communications technology'. Software is also eligible expenditure where it is a capital purchase

CAPITAL ALLOWANCES FOR PLANT AND MACHINERY

Capital allowances for plant and machinery are currently through:
- Full Expensing
- the Annual Investment Allowance (AIA), and
- other capital allowances, such as First Year Allowances (FYAs) and Writing Down Allowances (WDAs)

Note that capital allowances are not scaled down according to when in the Chargeable Accounting Period (CAP) an asset is bought. If (for example) an asset is eligible for an 18% allowance, the full 18% is claimable whether the asset is bought in the first month of the CAP or the last month.

We will look at each of these allowances in turn, and see how they work.

Full Expensing

This allowance is only available for expenditure on qualifying assets incurred from 1 April 2023. It is a form of first year allowance, and it provides a capital allowance in the CAP in which the asset was acquired equal to 100% of the cost of the asset. It is available for the acquisition of virtually all **new** plant and machinery, **except cars**. There is **no limit** on the amount of Full Expensing allowance that can be claimed by a company.

The main situations where it **cannot** be claimed are

- acquisitions before 1 April 2023

- acquisitions of second-hand assets

- acquisitions of cars

example

A company acquired the following assets during the CAP year ended 31/12/2023:

- New machinery acquired before 1/4/2023   £300,000
- New machinery acquired after 1/4/2023   £800,000
- Used plant acquired after 1/4/2023   £100,000
- New lorries acquired after 1/4/2023   £250,000
- Cars acquired after 1/4/2023   £125,000

The Full Expensing allowance could be claimed on new machinery acquired after 1/4/2023 costing £800,000, and new lorries acquired after 1/4/2023 costing £250,000.

The total cost of £1,050,000 would be available as a 100% first year allowance, and £1,050,000 capital allowance could be claimed.

We will see later in this chapter how a Plant and Machinery capital allowance computation can be prepared that shows how this and other capital allowances are calculated and brought together.

Annual Investment Allowance (AIA)

This provides a very simple system for companies to claim capital allowances. The Annual Investment Allowance applies to virtually all new or used plant and machinery **except cars**, and provides an allowance of the whole amount spent on this plant and machinery, up to a total amount of £1,000,000.

Any acquisitions in a year that exceed the relevant limit are dealt with through the pooled system that we will look at shortly, and will then be eligible for other capital allowances.

The key features of the scheme are:

- it applies to the acquisition in the Chargeable Accounting Period of virtually all plant and machinery except cars

- it is available for the first £1,000,000 of qualifying expenditure per 12 month CAP

- the relevant limit is reduced proportionally if the CAP is less than 12 months (eg the limit is £750,000 for a nine month CAP)

- it gives a capital allowance equal to the whole of such expenditure, and this allowance can then be deducted in the calculation of adjusted trading profits

example

Suppose A Limited had adjusted trading profits (before capital allowances) of £1,900,000 for the CAP 1/1 /2023 to 31/12/2023.

If during the CAP it spent £120,000 on used plant and machinery, it could set the whole £120,000 against trading profits, giving a trading income assessment of £1,780,000.

or

If during the CAP it spent £1,045,000 on used plant and machinery, it could set £1,000,000 (the maximum) against trading profits, giving a trading income assessment of £900,000 before other capital allowances. The remaining £45,000 expenditure would be subject to capital allowance claims through the pooling system.

We will shortly look at how this works and what allowances can be claimed.

In some cases groups of companies may not be entitled to the normal annual limit for each company in the group, but may be required to share the limit between the companies. This could occur if the companies shared premises or had similar activities.

pooled expenditure calculations

We have looked at the main features of two of the most important capital allowances for Plant and Machinery. We now need to see how 'pools' are used to show all the relevant calculations. The format that we will use is called a 'capital allowance computation', and you will need to be able to complete one in your examination.

The capital allowance computation uses pools to deal with brought forward balances, expenditure on assets, asset disposal proceeds, and claiming of the various types of allowance including Full Expensing and Annual Investment Allowance. The result of the computation is a total of capital allowance for Plant and Machinery claimed for the Chargeable Accounting Period, and any pool balances to be carried forward.

Each pool requires a separate calculation (shown in a separate column) in the capital allowance computation. Separate pools are used for:

■ a 'special rate pool' that is used for cars that have high emissions levels (over 50 g/km) and is also used for certain long-life assets and 'integral features'. The definition of 'high emissions levels' has decreased over recent years

■ the general (or 'main') pool for everything else, including cars of 50 g/km emissions or less all merged together

The pool workings will carry forward from one period to the next, and keep running totals of unrelieved expenditure.

The other capital allowances (apart from Full Expensing and AIA) that can be calculated and claimed through this system are as follows:

■ **100% First Year Allowances (FYAs)**. These are **only** available for **new zero-emission cars** (ie 0 g/km CO_2) and **new zero-emission goods vehicles**. This includes electric cars. This means that the whole cost of a new zero-emission car can be claimed as a capital allowance. This is separate to, and in addition to, any Full Expensing or Annual Investment Allowance claimed for other plant. Other cars (that aren't new and/or don't meet the definition of zero-emission) are not entitled to 100% First Year Allowances

■ **18% Writing Down Allowance (WDA)** is available on **main pool balances**

■ **6% Writing Down Allowance (WDA)** is available for the pool balance on the special rate pool

■ **Balancing Allowances** (or the opposite – a **balancing charge**) are calculated when a single asset pool is closed because the asset has been disposed of. It can also occur in the general pool if the business ceases, or when an asset that Full Expensing was claimed on is subsequently disposed of

carrying out a computation using pools

In order to follow logically through the process, it is best to deal with the elements in the following order, using as many pools as necessary:

■ **start** with the written down values brought forward from the previous period

■ **add** the eligible expenditure on any acquisitions that do not qualify for Full Expensing, other first year allowances or annual investment allowance. This will be expenditure on 'normal' cars (ie not new zero-emission) and will need to be analysed into:

– those over 50 g/km (these go into the special rate pool), and

– those between 1 g/km and 50 g/km (that go into the general pool)

– secondhand zero-emission cars also go into the general pool

- ■ **calculate** 100% Full Expensing first year allowance on any new qualifying plant and machinery acquired on or after 1/4/2023

- ■ **calculate** 100% first year allowances on any new zero-emission cars or other qualifying plant

- ■ **calculate** the annual investment allowance on qualifying expenditure. Where the expenditure exceeds the available AIA, add any remaining balance of expenditure into the relevant pool

- ■ **deduct** the proceeds of disposals (limited to the original cost) including assets on which AIA or FYA has previously been claimed

- ■ **calculate** the writing down allowances (WDAs) on the pool balances after the above transactions

- ■ **calculate** the written down values of each pool to be carried forward to the next Chargeable Accounting Period

- ■ **calculate** the total capital allowances that can be claimed

This is quite complicated, but once a few examples have been looked at it should become clearer. Let us first look at a fairly basic example so that we can get the idea of the way that it works.

example

The Simple Company Limited has a Chargeable Accounting Period running from 1 January 2023 to 31 December 2023. At the start of the period there was a brought forward balance of £26,000 in the general (main) pool from the previous year.

During the Chargeable Accounting Period y/e 31/12/2023, the Simple Company Ltd had the following transactions in plant and machinery:

Purchases (cost)

Used Plant & Machinery (bought March)	£1,015,000
Car (emissions 40 g/km)	£18,000

Disposals (proceeds)

Plant (main pool)	£5,000

The Simple Company Limited had adjusted trading profits (before capital allowances) for the CAP y/e 31/12/2023 of £1,750,000.

Required

(a) Calculate the total capital allowances claimable for the CAP.

(b) Calculate the assessable trading profits after deducting capital allowances.

Solution

(a) The capital allowance computation using the pool is built up as follows. The column on the right hand side is to collect and total the allowances. Note that allowances are deducted from the pool balances, but appear as positive figures in the capital allowances column.

		Main Pool	Capital Allowances
		£	£
WDV bf		26,000	
add			
Acquisitions without FYA or AIA:			
Car (40 g/km)		18,000	
Acquisitions qualifying for AIA:			
Plant & Machinery	1,015,000		
AIA Claimed	(1,000,000)		1,000,000
Balance into main pool		15,000	
less			
Proceeds of Disposals		(5,000)	
		54,000	
18% WDA		(9,720)	9,720
WDV cf		44,280	
Total Capital Allowances			1,009,720

Note the following important points:

The cost of the car enters the main pool. This is because it has an emission rating of 50 g/km or less.

The plant and machinery is entitled to annual investment allowance (AIA) of £1,000,000. Full Expensing is not available as the plant is used, and was bought before 1/4/2023. This calculation is carried out next, and the excess of £15,000 is added to the main pool. This £15,000 will form part of the balance of £54,000 that is entitled to 18% writing down allowance (WDA).

The proceeds on disposal are deducted from the pool before the writing down allowance (WDA) is calculated.

The total capital allowance is made up of the AIA and the WDA in this example.

(b) The assessable trading profit can now be calculated:

	£
Adjusted trading profits (before capital allowances)	1,750,000
less capital allowances	(1,009,720)
Assessable trading profit	740,280

claiming Full Expensing or Annual Investment Allowance

Although there is no limit on the amount that can be claimed through Full Expensing, there is an annual limit of £1,000,000 for the amount of Annual Investment Allowance claimed. However, Full Expensing cannot be claimed on used plant, nor can it be claimed on plant acquired before 1/4/2023.

Both allowances provide 100% capital allowance, and so when either allowance could be claimed for an asset, there is no immediate difference in the effect on tax whichever allowance is claimed. However, there is one important difference in the way that disposals of the assets on which claims were made are treated.

When assets on which Full Expensing was claimed are later disposed of, this will trigger an immediate balancing charge equal to the disposal proceeds, which is effectively the opposite to a capital allowance.

When assets on which Annual Investment Allowance was claimed are later disposed of the effect is a reduction in the pool balance equal to the disposal proceeds. This will typically delay the negative tax impact of the disposal. This will often be an advantage to the company, compared with the equivalent Full Expensing procedure.

Where a choice can be made between claiming Full Expensing or Annual Investment Allowance, then if a later disposal is anticipated, consideration should be given to the different disposal tax implications.

small pools allowance

Where the subtotal in either the main pool or the special rate pool at the end of a CAP is £1,000 or less, the whole amount can be claimed as a 'small pools allowance' instead of the normal writing down allowance. The £1,000 limit relates to the pool balance that the writing down allowance would normally be calculated on.

After the small pools allowance has been claimed, there will be no balance in the relevant pool to carry forward to the next CAP.

We will now use a slightly more complex Case Study to see how the capital allowance computation works in more detail.

SPENDER PLC:
PLANT AND MACHINERY CAPITAL ALLOWANCES

Spender plc has a Chargeable Accounting Period running from 1 April 2023 to 31 March 2024.

At the start of the period there was a balance of £48,000 brought forward from the previous year in the main pool.

During the CAP y/e 31/3/2024, Spender plc had the following transactions in plant and machinery:

Purchases (cost)

New machinery	£2,000,000
Used equipment	£232,000
Used lorries	£867,000
New zero-emission car	£28,000
Car (emissions of 100 g/km)	£19,000

Disposals (proceeds)

Plant (main pool)	£10,000

Spender plc had adjusted trading profits (before capital allowances) of £6,500,000 for the CAP y/e 31/3/2024.

required

(a) Calculate the total capital allowances claimable for the CAP.

(b) Calculate the assessable trading profits after deducting capital allowances.

solution

(a) Of the expenditure during the CAP, only the new machinery costing £2,000,000 is eligible for the full expensing first year allowance.

The used equipment and used lorries are eligible for AIA, but their total cost of £1,099,000 exceeds the annual limit of £1,000,000.

This expenditure in excess of the AIA allowance will be added to the main pool and be eligible for writing down allowances (WDA) at 18%.

The new zero-emission car will be eligible for 100% first year allowance.

The car with emissions of 100 g/km will join the special rate pool, and it will be entitled to writing down allowances of 6%.

The capital allowances computation is completed as follows. Note that the acquisitions and disposals are detailed in the left column, and amounts transferred to the pools and/or the capital allowance column. Allowances show as positive figures in the capital allowance column, but as negative figures in the other columns.

The final written down values carried forward (WDV cf) will be used as brought forward figures at the start of the next CAP.

	AIA £	FYA £	Full Expensing £	Main Pool £	Special Rate Pool £	Total Allowances £
WDV bf				48,000		
Car (100 g/km)					19,000	
New machinery			2,000,000			
Full Expensing			(2,000,000)			2,000,000
Used equipment	232,000					
Used lorries	867,000					
AIA Excess	(1,000,000) (99,000)			99,000		1,000,000
New car (0 g/km)		28,000				
FYA		(28,000)				28,000
Disposals				(10,000)		
Pools Sub Totals				137,000	19,000	
18% WDA				(24,660)		24,660
6% WDA					(1,140)	1,140
WDV cf				112,340	17,860	
Total Capital Allowances						3,053,800

Note that here we have used a format that uses analysis columns for AIA, FYA and Full Expensing additions and allowances.

(b) Following the capital allowances computation, the assessable trading profit can now be calculated:

	£
Adjusted trading profits (before capital allowances)	6,500,000
less capital allowances	(3,053,800)
Assessable trading profit	3,446,200

CAPITAL ALLOWANCES FOR SHORT CAPS

So far in this chapter we have examined the way that capital allowances for plant and machinery are calculated for Chargeable Accounting Periods of twelve months.

It is, however, possible to have CAPs for less than twelve months, and this can arise either:

- if the accounts are prepared for a period of less than twelve months, or

- where accounts are prepared for a period exceeding twelve months, and are divided into two CAPs, one for the first twelve months, and another for the balance, which will be for less than twelve months

In each of these situations, the impact on capital allowances for plant and machinery in the short CAP is as follows:

- First Year Allowances (including Full Expensing), Balancing Allowances and Balancing Charges are unaffected and are calculated as normal

- Writing Down Allowances are time-apportioned based on the short CAP

- the Annual Investment Allowance maximum limit is time-apportioned based on the short CAP.

DEALING WITH THE ACCOUNTS FOR A LONG PERIOD

As we saw in the last chapter, where we have accounts that are prepared for a long period, the procedure is:

- the accounting profits for the long period are adjusted in one computation, before deducting capital allowances

- this adjusted profits figure is then time-apportioned into the two CAPs

- capital allowances are calculated separately for each CAP

- each CAP's adjusted profit is then finalised by deducting the capital allowances that have been calculated for that CAP

We can now examine the issues involved in creating two capital allowance computations, one for each CAP within a long period for which accounts were prepared. The points to note are:

- each acquisition and disposal of assets needs to be allocated to the correct CAP, and incorporated in the appropriate computation
- the written down values at the end of the first CAP will become the brought forward amounts at the start of the second CAP
- the rules regarding time-apportionment of WDAs for short CAPs as described above need to be used in the second CAP

Now that we have seen all the principles explained, we can use a Case Study to illustrate the way they work.

Case Study

CHOPPITT PLC:
DEALING WITH ACCOUNTS FOR A LONG PERIOD

Choppitt plc has produced a set of accounts for the period 1/9/2022 to 31/12/2023. The adjusted trading profit for the 16-month period has already been produced from the accounts, and provides a profit of £1,600,000, before any capital allowances are taken account of.

The plant and machinery capital allowance computation for the CAP y/e 31/8/2022 provided carried forward written down values as follows:

- main pool   £50,000

Analysis of the accounts reveals that the following assets were acquired or disposed of during the 16-month period:

1/4/2023	disposal of plant for £2,000 (original cost £20,000)
1/10/2023	acquisition of secondhand BMW car for £17,500 (45 g/km)
1/11/2023	acquisition of new plant costing £370,000

required

1   State the periods for the two CAPs.

2   Calculate the plant and machinery capital allowances for each of the two CAPs.

3   Calculate the trading income assessments for each of the two CAPs.

solution

1 The CAPs will be:

1/9/2022 - 31/8/2023	(12 months)
1/9/2023 - 31/12/2023	(4 months)

2 To calculate the plant and machinery capital allowances we will need to prepare two computations, one for each CAP.

Each one will incorporate the acquisitions and disposals that occur in that CAP. Within the CAP for the 12 months ending 31/8/2023 is disposal of plant.

There are no acquisitions of plant and machinery in this period that can be used to claim Full Expensing or annual investment allowance (AIA). The maximum AIA would have been £1,000,000.

The capital allowance computation is as follows:

CAP FOR THE 12 MONTHS ENDING 31/8/2023		
	Main pool	**Capital allowances**
	£	£
WDV bf	50,000	
Disposals:		
Plant	(2,000)	
Sub Total	48,000	
WDA 18%	(8,640)	8,640
WDV cf	39,360	
Total Capital Allowances		8,640

Within the four-month CAP ending 31/12/2023 are the acquisition of plant, and the BMW car.

The new plant is eligible for the Full Expensing FYA since it was acquired after 1/4/2023. If AIA were claimed instead, it would be limited to £1,000,000 x 4/12 = £333,333

Note that the annual WDA % for the main pool is 18%. The 18% is reduced to 4/12 since it is a short CAP.

CAP FOR THE 4 MONTHS TO 31/12/2023		
	Main pool	**Capital allowances**
	£	£
WDV bf	39,360	
add		
Acquisitions without FYA or AIA:		
Car (45 g/km)	17,500	
Acquisitions qualifying for Full Expensing:		
Plant £370,000		
£(370,000)		370,000
	56,860	
WDA 18% × 4/12	(3,412)	3,412
WDV cf	53,448	
Total Capital Allowances		373,412

3 Calculation of trading income assessments.

Firstly the adjusted trade profits are time-apportioned:

CAP 1/9/2022 to 31/8/2023   £1,600,000 × 12/16   = £1,200,000

CAP 1/9/2023 to 31/12/2023   £1,600,000 × 4/16   = £400,000

Capital allowances are then deducted from the adjusted profit for each CAP:

	1/9/22 – 31/8/23	1/9/23 – 31/12/23
	£	£
Adjusted profit	1,200,000	400,000
Capital allowances:		
P & M	(8,640)	(373,412)
Trading Income	1,191,360	26,588

CAPITAL ALLOWANCES WHEN COMPANIES CEASE TRADING

When a company ceases trading, the capital allowances in the final CAP are subject to a special approach, as follows:

- there can be **no** WDA, FYA, Full Expensing or AIA in this final CAP
- all remaining assets will have been disposed of by the company, with any proceeds brought into the computation as normal
- there can be no written down values to carry forward in **any** pools, so the pools must be closed by using balancing allowances or balancing charges to bring all the pool balances to zero

As the only capital allowances will be balancing allowances or charges, the length of the final CAP will not cause any complications. This is because balancing allowances and balancing charges are unaffected by short CAPs as we discussed a little earlier.

STRUCTURES AND BUILDINGS ALLOWANCE

Structures and buildings allowance (SBA) is a separate capital allowance to the plant and machinery allowances that we have been discussing so far. It follows different rules, and it does not form part of the plant and machinery capital allowance computation.

The structures and buildings allowance is calculated as **3% per year** of the **eligible expenditure** on a structure or building that is used for a **qualifying activity**.

Eligible expenditure on a new building is based on construction costs, including design fees and site preparation. It does not include the cost of the land, nor stamp duty, nor the cost of obtaining planning permission. Any costs which qualify as plant and machinery (for example, fixed machinery) cannot also qualify for structures and buildings allowance.

If a used building is bought, then the eligible expenditure will be limited to the amount that the previous owner was able to base their claim for SBA on.

The definition of a **qualifying activity** is quite broad, and includes 'any trades, professions and vocations' – i.e. business use. It does not include residential use.

The allowance can first be claimed on a building at the **later of**

- the date when it was first used for a qualifying activity, and
- the date when payment is made for the eligible expenditure.

The allowance can then be claimed at 3% per year for 33 1/3 years from that date, provided it is still being used for a qualifying activity.

Where the allowance is claimed in a CAP that is shorter than 12 months, the 3% is reduced by time-apportionment for that CAP.

If the date that the allowance is first claimed is part way through a CAP, then the amount claimed in that CAP will be time-apportioned.

example

A company paid £1,100,000 for a newly constructed building (excluding land) on 30 June 2023. It started using the building for a qualifying purpose on 1 August 2023.

During the CAP year ended 31/12/2023 the company could claim

3% x £1,100,000 x 5/12 = £13,750   (based on 1 August to 31 December)

During the CAP year ended 31/12/2024 the company could claim

   3% x £1,100,000   = £33,000

This amount could be claimed each full year, provided it was still used for a qualifying purpose until 30/11/2056 when the allowance runs out because the eligible expenditure has all been claimed. This is because 3% x 33 1/3 = 100%.

The allowance for the company will cease if the structure or building is

- sold, or

- demolished, or

- no longer used for a qualifying purpose.

When this happens, the allowance simply stops from that date. There is no clawback of previous claims or balancing charge.

If the building is sold and bought by a company or individual that uses it for a qualifying purpose, then the new owner will take over the same allowance for the remaining years. Note that this is based on the original eligible expenditure by the first claimant, not how much the new owner paid.

example

To continue the earlier example, suppose the building was sold on 1 January 2025 to a new owner for £1,500,000, who also used it for a qualifying activity.

The purchase price would be ignored for the calculation of the allowance, and the new owner would claim 3% x £1,100,000 = £33,000 per year from 1/1/2025.

Chapter Summary

■   Capital allowances are available on certain non-current (fixed) assets, and act for tax computation purposes as an alternative to depreciation, which is never allowable as tax-deductible (set off against tax).

■   The main type of capital allowance is for 'plant and machinery'.

■   Plant and machinery includes vehicles, computers, and various other assets.

■   A 'Full Expensing' first year allowance of 100% eligible expenditure is available for most new plant and machinery acquired from 1/4/2023, except cars.

■   An annual investment allowance is available for the whole cost of virtually all plant and machinery, except cars, up to a maximum of £1,000,000 for 12-month periods.

■   Allowances include 100% first year allowances for new zero-emission cars, and zero-emission goods vehicles. There are also writing down allowances at various rates depending on the circumstances.

■   Most assets are merged together or 'pooled' in the capital allowance computation. Balancing allowances and charges occur in the general pool and special rate pool when the business ceases.

■   When capital allowances are calculated for a Chargeable Accounting Period of less than twelve months, any writing down allowances are time-apportioned. The AIA limit is also time-apportioned.

■   First year allowances and balancing allowances and charges are unaffected by short CAPs. Where the accounts for a company have been prepared for a period of over 12 months, the two CAPs that result will each require a separate capital allowance computation. Non-current asset acquisitions and disposals will need to be allocated to the correct CAP before these capital allowance computations are carried out.

■   Structures and buildings allowance (SBA) is separate from plant and machinery allowances. It is calculated at 3% of eligible expenditure on property used for qualifying activities, on a straight-line basis.

Key Terms	**capital allowance**	the term used for allowances that reduce taxable profit for a Chargeable Accounting Period, resulting from the acquisition and use of certain non-current assets
	Chargeable Accounting Period (CAP)	the period for which the profits chargeable to Corporation Tax must be calculated. It is the same as the period for which the company produces financial accounts, unless that period is for more than twelve months. In that case the financial accounting period is divided into two CAPs
	plant and machinery	one of the major non-current asset categories for capital allowance purposes. It includes vehicles and computers
	full expensing allowance	an allowance available at 100% of most new plant (excluding cars) acquired from 1/4/2023
	annual investment allowance (AIA)	this is an allowance that can be claimed against the whole cost of most plant and machinery, with the exception of cars. The maximum is £1,000,000 for a 12-month period
	first year allowances	first year allowances are available at 100% for new zero-emission cars, and zero-emission goods vehicles
	writing down allowances (WDA)	these allowances are available at a percentage of the pool value for plant and machinery. This percentage is time-apportioned for short CAPs
	written down value (WDV)	this term relates to the balance at the end of a CAP that remains in a plant and machinery pool. It represents the part of the pool value that has not yet been claimed as allowances, and is carried forward to the next CAP
	balancing allowance	a balancing allowance or balancing charge will occur in all pools when a company ceases trading
	balancing charge	this charge is the opposite of a balancing allowance, and occurs when the disposal proceeds are more than the written down value (unrelieved expenditure) of the pool. It is in effect a reclaiming of excess allowances previously obtained. It also applies to the disposal of an asset on which full expensing was previously claimed
	structures and buildings allowance	an allowance available at 3% of eligible expenditure on property used for qualifying activities

Activities

3.1   A company has a 12-month CAP from 1/1/2023 to 31/12/2023. At the start of the period the written down value in the main pool was £21,000.

During the CAP the company had the following transactions in plant and machinery:

Acquisitions (Costs):
Car (emissions 40 g/km)	£16,000
Used Plant	£993,000
Van (used)	£10,000

Disposals (Proceeds – less than original cost):
Machinery	£2,000

Required:

Calculate the total capital allowances for the CAP.

3.2   The Capital Company Limited has a twelve month Chargeable Accounting Period running from 1/4/2023 to 31/3/2024. The adjusted trading profit for this CAP has already been calculated at £154,000 before deduction of capital allowances for plant and machinery.

The capital allowance computation for the last CAP closed with written down value as follows:

Main pool	£60,000

During the CAP the following assets were acquired and disposed of:

30/4/2023	a new fork-lift truck was bought for £30,000
31/7/2023	a new BMW car was bought for £24,000 (emissions 45 g/km)
31/7/2023	a new computer system was bought for £5,000
31/12/2023	a machine in the main pool was sold for £3,000

Disposal proceeds were less than original cost.

Required:

• Using a plant and machinery capital allowance computation, calculate the total allowances for the CAP year ended 31/3/2024.

• Calculate the assessable trading income for the CAP year ended 31/3/2024.

3.3 The Middle Company Limited has a 12-month CAP from 1/10/2022 to 30/9/2023. At the start of the period the written down value in the main pool was £10,000, and there was also a special rate pool with a balance of £2,800.

During the CAP the company had the following transactions in plant and machinery:

Acquisitions (Costs):

Plant (new)	£1,196,750	bought 1/5/2023
Machinery (new)	£12,000	bought 1/6/2023

Disposals (Proceeds – less than cost):

Machinery in main pool	£3,500

Required:

Calculate the total capital allowances, assuming the maximum is claimed.

3.4 Solvitt plc has produced a set of accounts for the period 1/12/2021 to 28/2/2023. The adjusted trading profit for the 15-month period has already been computed as £480,000, before any capital allowances are taken account of.

The plant and machinery capital allowance computation for the CAP y/e 30/11/2021 provided carried forward written down values as follows:

Main pool	£60,000
Special rate pool	£14,000

Analysis of the accounts reveals that the following assets were acquired or disposed of during the 15-month period.

1/8/2022	Disposal of plant for £4,000 (original cost £30,000)
1/11/2022	Acquisition of secondhand Ford car for £16,000 (emissions 63 g/km)
1/1/2023	Acquisition of used plant costing £45,000

Required:

- State the periods for the two CAPs that need to be formed.
- State the AIA limit for each CAP.
- Calculate the plant and machinery capital allowances for each of the two CAPs.
- Calculate the trading income assessments for each of the two CAPs.

3.5 Tuffwun Limited has produced a set of accounts for the period 1/4/2023 to 31/1/2024. The adjusted trading profit for the 10-month period has already been produced from the accounts, and provides a profit of £1,510,000, before any capital allowances are taken account of.

Tuffwun Limited's plant and machinery capital allowance computation for the CAP y/e 31/3/2023 provided carried forward written down values as follows:

Main pool	£90,000
Special rate pool	£13,000

Analysis of the accounts reveals that the following assets were acquired or disposed of during the 10-month period:

Acquisition of new 'zero-emission' car for £20,000

Acquisition of a BMW car for £27,000 (emissions 189 g/km)

Disposal of plant for £1,000 (original cost £10,000)

Acquisition of new plant costing £857,500

Required:

- Calculate the plant and machinery capital allowances for Tuffwun Limited for the CAP to 31/1/2024.

- Calculate the trading income assessment for Tuffwun Limited for the CAP to 31/1/2024.

3.6 Zee Ltd has its CAPs ending on 31 December each year.

On 1 June 2023 Zee Ltd paid a developer £2,650,000 for a new factory, including land valued at £400,000. It moved into the factory and started using it for its engineering business on 1 September 2023.

Calculate the structures and buildings allowance that can be claimed by Zee Ltd for 2023, and for 2024.

4 Corporation Tax – chargeable gains

this chapter covers...

In this chapter we learn about how chargeable gains (and the opposite – capital losses) are calculated. These gains then form part of the taxable total profits (TTP) for a limited company.

We start by examining the basis of assessment, including what constitutes the disposal of an asset. We then learn how to calculate gains using the basic format, before going on to look at some special situations.

The situations that we examine further are:

■   improvement expenditure

■   matching rules for shares

■   bonus and rights share issues

Finally we examine a deferral relief that can be opted for when a company buys assets in certain categories within a defined time of disposing of an asset. This 'rollover relief' has the effect of postponing the impact of the gain on the first asset.

INTRODUCTION TO CHARGEABLE GAINS

A chargeable gain (or its opposite – a capital loss) occurs when a company disposes of certain assets that it has previously acquired. The gain is then brought into the Corporation Tax computation. It does not apply to a trading situation, where items are regularly bought and sold to make a profit. Such profits would be assessed as trading income, as we have already seen. The assets that can form chargeable gains will often be non-current (fixed) assets or investments that the company has acquired outside of its trading activities. A chargeable gain often applies to the sale of an asset that may have been owned for quite some time.

In addition to applying to the business assets of companies, chargeable gains can also arise for individuals who are subject to Capital Gains Tax on the disposal of both personal assets and business assets. In this book, however, we are only going to examine how disposals of business assets are taxed. In this chapter we will examine the way that companies' chargeable gains are subject to Corporation Tax, and later in this book we will look at how Capital Gains Tax applies to the disposal of business assets by individuals.

Gains on the disposal of personal assets are dealt with in Osborne Books' *Personal Tax* Tutorial and Workbook.

a note for those familiar with Capital Gains Tax for individuals

Although there are similarities between Capital Gains Tax for individuals and the treatment of chargeable gains for companies under Corporation Tax, there are also **significant differences**. If you have already studied personal taxation you should be very careful to study the way in which the gains of companies are taxed. Do not be lulled into a false sense of security by the similarities to the system that you have already studied.

The following main differences between Capital Gains Tax for individuals and chargeable gains for companies will now be highlighted in advance so that you can appreciate their impact. In calculating the chargeable gains of companies:

- there is no annual exempt amount

- there is an indexation allowance, claimed up to the earlier of the date of disposal or December 2017 for acquisitions before that date

- the matching rules for shares are different from those for individuals

These are important differences, and can cause confusion.

basis of assessment

Chargeable gains are calculated according to the same Chargeable Accounting Periods (CAPs) as are used for the rest of the Corporation Tax computation. The basis of assessment is the chargeable gains less capital losses arising from disposals that occur during the CAP. We will look at how losses are dealt with a little later in this chapter. The main issue to understand at this point is that the chargeable gain that is brought into the Corporation Tax computation is based on the total (or aggregate) of gains that have occurred during the CAP, and that a gain can only arise when a disposal has taken place.

disposals

A disposal arises when an asset is:

- sold (or part of it is sold)

- given away

- lost, or

- destroyed

Most of the situations that we will deal with will be based on the sale of an asset.

CHARGEABLE AND EXEMPT ASSETS

For a chargeable gain or capital loss to arise, the asset that has been disposed of must be a 'chargeable' asset. Disposals of exempt assets cannot form chargeable gains or capital losses. Instead of there being a long list of the assets that are chargeable, there is a fairly short list of assets that are exempt. The simple rule is that if an asset is not exempt, then it must be chargeable!

Chargeable business assets that are popular in tasks include:

- land and buildings

- shares

You must remember that these are only examples – all assets are chargeable unless they are exempt.

exempt assets

The following is a list of the main **exempt assets** that relate to companies:

- trading inventory (as discussed earlier, this is part of the trading profit)

- cars

- chattels bought and sold for £6,000 or less (chattels are tangible moveable property)

- Government Securities (also known as 'gilts', these are a form of investment)

- animals (for example, racehorses)

CHARGEABLE GAINS AND CORPORATION TAX

Where, during a CAP, there are several disposals that result in chargeable gains, these are aggregated and the result brought into the Corporation Tax computation. This total chargeable gain then forms part of the 'taxable total profits' (TTP), along with trading profits as Trading Income and any income from investments. The Corporation Tax is then calculated on the total profits, as we will see in the next chapter.

If any disposals result in capital losses, then these are set against any chargeable gains relating to the same CAP. Provided the net result is a chargeable gain, this amount is brought into the Corporation Tax computation as described above. If the losses exceed the chargeable gains of the same CAP, then the result is that:

- no chargeable gains are brought into the TTP computation, and

- the net capital loss is carried forward to be set against the chargeable gain that arises in the next CAP (and so on if necessary until all the loss is utilised)

Note that **capital losses cannot be set against any other profits** (eg from trading or investment) in the Corporation Tax computation, but must be carried forward against future chargeable gains.

We must now turn our attention to how to calculate the chargeable gain or loss on each separate disposal.

THE COMPUTATION OF EACH GAIN

Each disposal of a chargeable asset requires a calculation to determine the amount of any gain or loss. This computation follows a standard format that is in effect a 'mini' statement of profit or loss (income statement) for the item disposed of.

There are some minor variations to this format in particular circumstances, as we will see later. The basic format is shown on the next page:

Computation of a chargeable gain	
	£
Proceeds on disposal	X
less	
Incidental costs of disposal	(x)
Net proceeds	X
less:	
Original cost	(x)
Incidental costs of acquisition	(x)
Unindexed gain	X
less	
Indexation allowance	(x)
Chargeable Gain	X

We will now look at the components of the individual gain computation in more detail.

proceeds on disposal

This normally refers to the amount that the asset was sold for, ie the selling price. However, there are some special situations where the figure used is different:

- if the asset is given away, or sold to a connected company or person at less than the market value, the market value is used in the computation instead of the actual amount received. Companies under the same control are connected with each other and with the person(s) controlling them

- if the asset is lost or destroyed then the asset will have been disposed of for zero proceeds, and zero will be used in the computation. The exception to this would be if an insurance claim had been made, in which case the claim proceeds would be used

incidental costs of disposal

These are the costs incurred by the company in selling the asset. Examples include advertising expenses, auction costs, or estate agent's fees for selling a property.

original cost, and incidental costs of acquisition

These relate to the amount paid to acquire the asset in the first place, plus any other costs incurred to buy it. Examples of these costs include legal fees and auction costs. We will examine later on in this chapter how to deal with expenditure that is incurred after purchase to improve the asset.

indexation allowance

This is a deduction that is used to compensate for the impact of inflation on the value of the asset. It works by using figures from the Retail Price Index (RPI) to calculate an inflation factor to multiply by the original cost and any other acquisition costs. This allows for general inflation of the **cost** between the date of acquisition and the **earlier** of the date of disposal and December 2017.

If acquisition was before December 2017, the indexation factor is calculated as:

$$\frac{(RPI \text{ at the date of disposal or December 2017} - RPI \text{ at the date of acquisition})}{RPI \text{ at the date of acquisition}}$$

Notice that indexation only takes account of inflation up to December 2017. If an asset is disposed of after this date, the RPI at December 2017 will be used instead of the RPI at the date of disposal. This is sometimes known as 'freezing' the indexation allowance.

If an asset was acquired **after December 2017** there will be no indexation allowance.

The result of this fraction is rounded to three decimal places before being multiplied by the **historical cost figure**.

A common error is to multiply the indexation factor by the unindexed gain instead of the cost. This is illogical.

If the fraction calculation produces a negative figure, because the RPI at disposal is lower than the RPI at acquisition, then no indexation is applied. This would occur if there was deflation occurring between the two dates. This means that indexation can never increase a gain.

Note also that the indexation allowance cannot either:

- turn an unindexed gain into a loss, or

- increase the amount of an unindexed loss

This means that the indexation allowance cannot be a larger amount than the unindexed gain that it follows in the computation. If the figure before indexation is applied is a loss, then there can be no indexation allowance at all.

We will now use a Case Study to show how the computation is carried out.

Note that the RPI figures are shown in the Tax Data section at the beginning of this book. The figures that we need in this Case Study are, however, repeated here for convenience. **You will normally be provided with the indexation factor itself** in an assessment.

<table>
<tr><td></td></tr>
</table>

THE SIMPLE COMPANY LIMITED: CALCULATING A CHARGEABLE GAIN

The Simple Company Limited bought a retail shop in August 1990. The company paid £59,000 for the shop, and also paid legal fees of £1,000 at the same time to arrange the purchase. The shop was sold in April 2023. The company prepares its accounts annually to 31 December, and the sale of the shop was the only chargeable disposal that the company made in 2023. It had no capital losses brought forward.

We will assume three different selling prices for the sale of the shop. In each case the estate agent's fees for the sale were £3,000, and the company incurred further legal fees of £2,000.

1   Assume that the company sold the shop for £240,000
2   Assume that the company sold the shop for £75,000
3   Assume that the company sold the shop for £58,000

required

Using the RPI figures of 128.1 for August 1990 and 278.1 for December 2017, calculate the chargeable gain or capital loss resulting from the disposal of the shop (to the nearest £) for each of the situations 1, 2 and 3. Notice that because the disposal was after December 2017, the December 2017 RPI will be used, not the April 2023 RPI.

Also state the amount of chargeable gain to be brought into the TTP for the CAP year ended 31/12/2023 for each situation, and explain how any capital loss should be dealt with.

solution

Option 1	£
Proceeds on disposal	240,000
less:	
Incidental costs of disposal	(5,000)
Net proceeds	235,000
less:	
Original cost	(59,000)
Incidental costs of acquisition	(1,000)
Unindexed gain	175,000
less:	
Indexation allowance*	(70,260)
Chargeable Gain	104,740

*the indexation factor is calculated as:

$$\frac{278.1 - 128.1}{128.1} = 1.171 \text{ (rounded to three decimal places)}$$

The indexation factor is multiplied by the costs incurred in August 1990 of £59,000 + £1,000 = £60,000:

1.171 × £60,000 = £70,260

The chargeable gain of £104,740 would form part of the TTP for the CAP for the year ended 31/12/2023.

Option 2	£
Proceeds on disposal	75,000
less:	
Incidental costs of disposal	(5,000)
Net proceeds	70,000
less:	
Original cost	(59,000)
Incidental costs of acquisition	(1,000)
Unindexed gain	10,000
less:	
Restricted indexation allowance*	(10,000)
Chargeable Gain	Nil

*Here the indexation allowance that would be calculated as £70,260 (as in option 1) is restricted to the amount of the unindexed gain of £10,000, so that it will not turn an unindexed gain into a loss.

Since there is neither a gain nor a loss, there is no figure to form part of the TTP for the CAP for the year ended 31/12/2023.

Option 3	£
Proceeds on disposal	58,000
less:	
Incidental costs of disposal	(5,000)
Net proceeds	53,000
less:	
Original cost	(59,000)
Incidental costs of acquisition	(1,000)
Unindexed loss	(7,000)
less:	
Indexation allowance*	Nil
Capital Loss	(7,000)

*Here there is no indexation allowance since there is an unindexed loss that cannot be increased through indexation.

Since there is a capital loss, and no chargeable gains in the CAP to set it against, there is no figure to form part of the TTP for the CAP y/e 31/12/2023. The capital loss of £7,000 will be carried forward to set against chargeable gains in the next CAP.

links with capital allowances

As we saw in the last chapter, capital allowances are available for 'plant and machinery' and 'structures and buildings'. The following rules apply to the disposal of non-current assets where capital allowances have been claimed on the asset:

■ where plant and machinery is sold for less than it cost, the only tax implication is through plant and machinery capital allowance computations. A capital loss will not arise

■ where structures and buildings allowance (SBA) has been claimed on an asset that is subsequently disposed of, the amount of SBA already claimed is added to the disposal proceeds, and this will have the effect of increasing a gain (or reducing a loss). Unless SBA is specifically mentioned in a task, you can assume that none has been claimed

IMPROVEMENT EXPENDITURE

Where expenditure after acquisition is used to enhance an asset, and the asset is then disposed of in this improved condition, the improvement expenditure forms an allowable cost in the computation.

The expenditure must be of a 'capital' nature, and examples of this could include extending a building or having an antique professionally restored. The improvement expenditure will also attract indexation allowance if it occurs before 31/12/17. This would run from the date the improvement expenditure was incurred until the earlier of the date of disposal or December 2017. A situation could therefore arise where two (or more) indexation allowances were deducted in the computation, each with different start dates, but all with the same end date. This is shown in the diagram below.

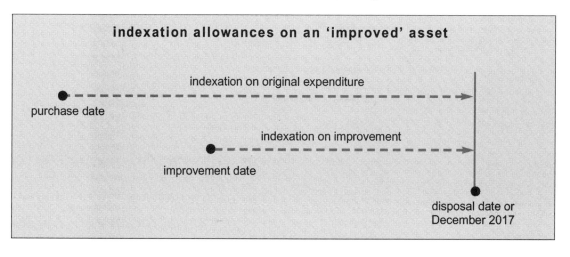

indexation allowances on an 'improved' asset

indexation on original expenditure

purchase date

indexation on improvement

improvement date

disposal date or December 2017

The following example illustrates how this works in practice:

example: chargeable gain involving improvement expenditure

Ledger and Company Limited bought an office building for £60,000 in September 1984. In January 1990 the company spent £40,000 extending the property. The company sold the building in April 2023 for £400,000.

The indexation factors are:

September 1984 to December 2017   2.086

January 1990 to December 2017   1.327

The calculation is as follows:

	£
Proceeds	400,000
less:	
original cost	(60,000)
improvement expenditure	(40,000)
Unindexed gain	300,000
less:	
indexation allowance on original cost	
2.086 × £60,000	(125,160)
indexation allowance on extension	
1.327 × £40,000	(53,080)
Chargeable Gain	121,760

If the asset was acquired and improved after December 2017 then there will be no indexation allowance.

We will now present a Case Study to consolidate an understanding of the main issues that we have covered in this chapter so far.

Case Study

INN CREASE LIMITED: USING SPECIAL RULES

Inn Crease Limited runs a chain of hotels and pubs. During the CAP y/e 31/12/2023 the company made the disposals listed below.

The company has capital losses brought forward from the previous CAP of £20,000.

disposals:

- The company sold an office building in March 2023 for £200,000. The building was bought in September 1995 for £60,000, and extended in June 2000 at a cost of £40,000.

- The company sold ten identical shoe-cleaning machines from its hotels for £100 each in January 2023. The machines had been bought for £500 each in January 1996, and plant and machinery capital allowances had been claimed on them through the main pool.

- The company sold 1,000 ordinary shares in Gloxxo plc for a total of £15,000 in March 2023. The shares had been bought for £6.00 each in September 1995. These had been the only shares that it owned in Gloxxo plc.

The indexation factors have been calculated as follows:

September 1995 - December 2017	0.847
June 2000 - December 2017	0.625

required

- Calculate the chargeable gain or capital loss on each applicable disposal.
- Calculate the total chargeable gain that will be used in the taxable total profits computation for the CAP y/e 31/12/2023.

solution

Office building

	£
Proceeds	200,000
less cost	(60,000)
Improvement expenditure	(40,000)
less:	
indexation on cost	
£60,000 × 0.847	(50,820)
indexation on improvement	
£40,000 × 0.625	(25,000)
	———
Chargeable gain	24,180
	———

Shoe cleaning machines

The shoe cleaning machines are sold at a loss, and are therefore dealt with entirely through the plant and machinery capital allowances computation.

Shares	£
Proceeds	15,000
less cost	(6,000)
less indexation (0.847 × £6,000)	(5,082)
	———
Chargeable Gain	3,918
	———

Calculation of chargeable gain for taxable total profits computation

We can now bring the chargeable gains together, and deduct the capital loss brought forward.

	£
Office building	24,180
Shares	3,918
	28,098
Less capital loss brought forward	(20,000)
Chargeable gain to be used in taxable total profits computation	8,098

MATCHING RULES FOR SHARES

In the Case Study on the previous pages, shares are shown as chargeable assets, and the computation for the acquisition and subsequent disposal of a block of shares is the same as for other assets.

A complication can arise when various quantities of the same type of share in the same company are bought over a period of time and then sold. The problem faced is similar to that in any inventory valuation situation – how to determine which of the shares that were bought are deemed to be the ones that were sold.

The problem is solved in this situation by the application of strict **matching rules** – in other words, matching up the shares that have been sold with the shares originally held.

When shares are sold, the **matching process** is carried out by working through, in order, the following categories of acquisition, missing out any that do not apply, until all the shares sold have been matched. A separate chargeable gains computation is then used for each separate match.

- firstly, any shares bought on the **same** day that the disposal occurs are matched with that disposal

- secondly, any shares bought in the nine days **before the disposal** are matched with those disposed of

- finally, any remaining shares not yet matched are deemed to have come from the **'FA 1985 pool'** of shares. This is a device for merging and indexing shares ('FA 1985' stands for the 'Finance Act 1985' which established this procedure, explained on the next page)

The matching process is a little complicated, but forms a possible examination task. The most likely questions will involve shares matched to the FA 1985 pool because there are no very recent acquisitions.

Note that these matching rules for companies are different from the ones that relate to individuals that you may have studied.

Remember that this matching process only applies where there have been several purchases of the same type of shares in the same company. It does not apply to a mixture of different companies' shares, nor is it needed where a shareholding is bought and sold intact.

using the 'FA 1985 pool'

This device was introduced in the 1985 Finance Act, and merges (or 'pools') shares in the same company and of the same type together, and applies indexation allowances at the same time. As explained on the last page, it forms the last of the matching rules, and is used to calculate the cost of shares acquired earlier than nine days before disposal.

The pooling process is similar to the calculation of weighted average inventory valuations (as you have probably studied in Costing), but with the additional complication of indexation allowance.

The 'pool' needs to record accurate data:

- the number of shares in each transaction
- actual costs
- indexed costs

These form the three main columns of the pool working.

The pool commences with the first shares bought. The cost of these is then indexed up to the time when other shares are bought (or sold). These are added in, and the cumulative indexed cost is then re-indexed up to the date of the next share purchase or sale (or December 2017 if this is earlier). This process is repeated as often as necessary, with the last indexation occurring up to the disposal date of the shares for which we are working out the gain (or December 2017). The indexed balance in the pool is then used to calculate the cost of shares from the pool that are sold, by apportionment based on the number of shares.

We will now demonstrate how this works, using a numerical example.

example: using the FA 1985 pool

On 1/1/2023 Jay Limited sold 10,000 ordinary shares in WyeCo Ltd for £15 each, from its shareholding of 25,000. The shareholding had been built up as follows:

    1/1/1988 bought 17,000 shares for £5.00 each

    1/1/1993 bought 8,000 shares for £7.00 each

relevant indexation factors are:

    January 1988 to January 1993   0.335

    January 1993 to December 2017   1.017

Since there are no acquisitions on the day of disposal, nor the nine days before that, the whole of the disposal of 10,000 shares will be matched with the pool. The pool will be built up as follows, with the disposal deducted as the latest transaction:

	Number	Cost	Indexed cost
		£	£
1/1/1988 Purchase	17,000	85,000	85,000
Indexation to Jan 1993:			
£85,000 x 0.335			28,475
			113,475
1/1/1993 Purchase	8,000	56,000	56,000
			169,475
Indexation to December 2017:			
£169,475 x 1.017			172,356
Pool Totals:	25,000	141,000	341,831
less Disposal	(10,000)	(56,400)	(136,732)
Pool Balance after disposal	15,000	84,600	205,099

You should examine these workings carefully, and note the following:

- Indexation is applied to consecutive periods based on transaction dates or December 2017. Here the periods were:

    – January 1988 to January 1993

    – January 1993 to December 2017

- Purchases at cost are added to the cumulative indexed cost figure, and the combined amount is then re-indexed to the date of the next transaction.

- The cost figures for the disposal are a proportional amount of the pool costs before disposal, based on the number of shares.

(eg £341,831 × 10,000 / 25,000 = £136,732)

The computation for the disposal will now be as follows:

	£
Proceeds (10,000 × £15)	150,000
less cost	(56,400)
less indexation (£136,732 – £56,400)	(80,332)
Chargeable Gain	13,268

The cost and indexation figures are shown here separately, but would total the indexed cost amount shown in the pool workings (£56,400 + £80,332 = £136,732). This is shown this way in case the indexation needs to be restricted to avoid creating a loss.

If at some future date there was another disposal of shares from the pool then the pool balances remaining would be used to determine the cost of the shares in the further disposal.

BONUS AND RIGHTS ISSUES

dealing with bonus shares

Bonus shares are additional shares given free to shareholders, based on their current shareholding. This is sometimes called a 'scrip issue' and this process may be carried out as part of a capital restructuring of a company.

For chargeable gains purposes, the bonus shares are treated as if they were acquired at the same time as the original shares that generated the issue. For example, a company that owned 1,000 shares that were bought in January 2001 would be entitled to a further 200 shares if there were a bonus issue of 'one for five' shares. The total of 1,200 shares would be treated as bought in January 2001 for the amount paid for the 1,000 shares.

Bonus shares are added to the pool when they are received. Since no payment is made, there is no adjustment to the cost or indexed cost figures. The bonus share transaction date is not relevant for indexation purposes.

dealing with rights issues

A rights issue is when additional shares are sold to existing shareholders, usually at a special discounted price. For matching purposes, the shares that are bought in this way are treated as if they were bought with the original shares. However, any indexation that applies to rights issue shares will only apply from the date that they were paid for. Rights issue shares will join the pool and be treated like any other share purchase. Their cost will be added into the pool, and the date they were bought (if before December 2017) will be treated as a date to index to and from as usual.

Dealing with share transactions is one of the most complicated areas of study in this Unit, yet it is a likely assessment task. We will therefore use a further Case Study to consolidate understanding.

CHER THYME LIMITED:
MATCHING AND POOLING SHARES

Cher Thyme Limited has acquired the following quoted ordinary shares in AbCo Plc:

1/5/1985	1,000 shares at £4.00 each	£4,000
1/1/1990	Bonus issue of 1 for 4	
1/1/1992	1,750 shares at £4.20 each	£7,350
1/1/1995	Rights issue of 1 for 2 at £4.10 each	
1/12/2001	1,800 shares at £5.10 each	£9,180

On 8/12/2001 the company sold 1,000 of its shareholding of AbCo Plc

On 15/3/2023 the company sold a further 2,500 ordinary shares in AbCo Plc for £10.00 each.

required

1   Identify which shares would have already been matched against the disposal that took place on 8/12/2001.

2   State how the disposal of shares on 15/3/2023 will be matched against the acquisitions.

3   Calculate the total gain arising from the sale of shares that took place on 15/3/2023.

Indexation factors have already been calculated, and are as follows:

May 1985 - Jan 1992	0.424
Jan 1992 - Jan 1995	0.077
Jan 1995 - Dec 2001	0.188
Dec 2001 - December 2017	0.604

solution

1   The disposal of 1,000 shares on 8/12/2001 would have been matched with 1,000 of the 1,800 shares that were bought on 1/12/2001 for £5.10 each. This leaves 800 of that purchase to join the pool at that time.

2   Matching of the 15/3/2023 disposal of 2,500 shares will be against the pool, since there are no acquisitions on the same day, or any in the previous nine days.

3 To carry out the computation we must first build up the FA 1985 pool:

	Number	Cost	Indexed cost
		£	£
1/5/1985 Purchase	1,000	4,000	4,000
1/1/1990 Bonus Issue	250		
Indexation May 1985 to Jan 1992:			
£4,000 × 0.424			1,696
	1,250	–	5,696
1/1/1992 Purchase	1,750	7,350	7,350
	3,000	11,350	13,046
Indexation Jan 1992 to Jan 1995			
£13,046 × 0.077			1,005
1/1/1995 Rights issue 1 for 2	1,500	6,150	6,150
	4,500	17,500	20,201
Indexation Jan 1995 to Dec 2001:			
£20,201 × 0.188			3,798
1/12/2001 Purchase (Balance)	800	4,080	4,080
	5,300	21,580	28,079
Indexation Dec 2001 to Dec 2017:			
£28,079 × 0.604			16,960
Pool Totals	5,300	21,580	45,039
less Disposal	(2,500)	(10,179)	(21,245)
Pool Balance after disposal	2,800	11,401	23,794

	£
Proceeds (2,500 x £10)	25,000
less cost	(10,179)
less indexation (£21,245 – £10,179)	(11,066)
Chargeable Gain	3,755

ROLLOVER RELIEF

Rollover relief applies when one business asset is sold, and another is bought. It is a deferral relief, which means that it postpones the impact of a chargeable gain. Since a gain can be deferred more than once, provided the rules don't change in the future, gains can sometimes be postponed almost indefinitely.

Where one business asset is replaced with another, then the gain of the first may be rolled over (deferred) into the second, so that any eventual gain on the replacement asset would include the gain deferred from the first asset.

For example, suppose a qualifying asset, such as a warehouse, is sold for £200,000, incurring a gain of £50,000. Another qualifying asset is then bought for £220,000, and the gain on the first asset is rolled over into the second, which means no tax is payable on the gain at this time.

If the second asset is sold some time later, and incurs a 'normal' chargeable gain of £100,000, the deferred gain from the first asset will increase the total chargeable gain to £150,000.

Full deferral can only occur when all the proceeds of the first asset are invested in the replacement asset(s). Any part of the proceeds that are not reinvested in the second asset will form a chargeable gain immediately.

The replacement asset (or assets) must be acquired between one year before and three years after the sale of the first asset.

All assets must be in the categories listed below, but do not have to be likefor-like replacements for each other, nor even in the same category.

This is an abbreviated list based on the type of assets involved:

- land and buildings
- immovable plant and machinery

A company could, for example, sell land, and invest the proceeds in an office building and roll over the gain.

A possible assessment task involves rollover relief relating to land and buildings. You may be expected to recognise that rollover relief would benefit a company in a given situation, and calculate the position accordingly.

Companies can choose whether or not to use rollover relief.

The example on the next page illustrates how the system works.

example: rollover relief

Rollo and Company Limited purchased an office building in January 1992 for £300,000. The company sold the building in January 2023 for £800,000. A shop had been purchased for £950,000 in August 2022.

The indexation factor from January 1992 to December 2017 is 1.051.

The chargeable gain on the office building would be calculated as follows (initially ignoring any rollover relief).

	£
Proceeds	800,000
less cost	(300,000)
less indexation	
1.051 × £300,000	(315,300)
Chargeable Gain	184,700

Using rollover relief, all of this gain of £184,700 can be deferred, because all of the proceeds were invested in the shop – the shop was bought for more than £800,000. This means that there is no gain on the office building chargeable in the current CAP.

The deferral works by deducting the deferred gain of £184,700 from the purchase cost of the shop in the chargeable gains computation when the shop is ultimately disposed of.

This would make the revised 'cost' figure (£950,000 – £184,700) = £765,300. Any gain at disposal of the shop would therefore consequently be greater than if rollover relief had not been used.

If the shop had been purchased for less than £800,000, not all of the gain on the office building could have been deferred. For example, if the shop had been bought for £700,000, only £84,700 of the gain could be deferred and a £100,000 gain would be chargeable immediately.

Chapter Summary

■ Chargeable gains for companies are part of the taxable total profits (TTP). Such gains arise when chargeable assets are disposed of during the Chargeable Accounting Period (CAP). A disposal usually takes the form of the sale of the asset. All assets are chargeable unless they are exempt. Exempt assets include cars, government securities (gilts), and certain chattels.

■ Each disposal uses a separate computation that compares the proceeds or market value with the original cost of the asset. Indexation allowance is also deductible based on inflation from the time of acquisition up to the earlier of the date of disposal and December 2017. Losses are set off against gains before bringing the net figure into the taxable total profits computation. Where the net result is a capital loss, the amount is carried forward to set against chargeable gains arising in the next CAP. Where capital allowances have been claimed on an asset that is disposed of, capital losses cannot arise.

■ Improvement expenditure that is reflected in the asset when disposed of is an allowable cost. It also attracts indexation allowance from the date of expenditure up to the date of disposal or December 2017.

■ When shares of the same type in the same company are bought and sold at different times, matching rules are used to identify the shares disposed of. Firstly, shares bought on the day of disposal are matched. Secondly, those bought in the nine days before disposal are matched. Thirdly, acquisitions are pooled (including indexation) and matched. This is known as the FA 1985 (Finance Act 1985) pool.

■ Bonus and rights issues are treated as acquired at the time of the shares that they are derived from for matching purposes. They can both appear as part of the FA 1985 pool.

■ Rollover relief relates to certain categories of assets. It can defer a chargeable gain where the company reinvests all or part of the proceeds of disposal in further assets. The full deferral of a gain can only occur when all of the proceeds are reinvested.

chargeable gains	these can arise when companies dispose of chargeable assets. Chargeable Gains form part of the taxable total profits (TTP)
capital loss	this is effectively a negative chargeable gain. It results when the allowable costs of an asset exceed the sale proceeds (or market value). Indexation cannot be used to increase a loss. A capital loss is used by setting it against a gain in the same CAP, or if this is not possible, by carrying it forward to set against chargeable gains in the next available CAP
disposal	a disposal for Capital Gains Tax purposes is the sale, gift, loss or destruction of an asset
chargeable asset	this term is used to describe assets, the disposal of which can result in a chargeable gain or capital loss. All assets are chargeable unless they are exempt
exempt asset	this is an asset that is not a chargeable asset. Exempt assets include cars, gilts, and some chattels
chattel	a tangible, moveable asset
net proceeds	the proceeds from the sale of an asset, less any incidental costs of selling the asset
unindexed gain	the net proceeds (or market value in some situations) less the original cost of the asset and any other allowable costs incurred. It is the subtotal of the gain computation before indexation allowance is deducted
indexation allowance	an amount that is deductible in the gain computation that compensates for the effect of inflation on the asset between acquisition and disposal (limited to December 2017). It uses the Retail Price Index to calculate a factor that is multiplied by the historical cost of the asset
improvement expenditure	this term relates to capital expenditure that enhances an asset. If the enhancement is still evident at disposal then the improvement expenditure is an allowable cost
matching rules for shares	these rules determine which acquisitions of shares are identified with each disposal

bonus shares   shares issued at no cost to shareholders, the number of shares being based on their current shareholding

rights issue   shares issued by a company to its existing shareholders at a special price

rollover relief   a deferral relief available to businesses (including companies). It has the effect of postponing a chargeable gain when the proceeds of disposal have been reinvested in further assets

Activities

4.1 Analyse the following list of assets into those that are chargeable assets and those that are exempt.

		Chargeable	Exempt
(a)	Antique painting sold for £10,000		
(b)	An office block		
(c)	Shares in CIC plc		
(d)	An industrial building		
(e)	A plot of land		
(f)	A car		
(g)	Government securities		
(h)	Trading stock		

4.2 April Limited bought an office block in May 1995 for £600,000 and sold it in January 2023 for £1,300,000. The company had no other disposals in the CAP y/e 31/12/2023. April Limited had a capital loss brought forward from the previous CAP of £15,000.

The indexation factor from May 1995 to December 2017 is 0.859.

Calculate the chargeable gain that will form part of the taxable total profits for April Limited for the CAP y/e 31/12/2023.

4.3 Cee Limited bought 200 ordinary shares in Zedco plc in August 1998 for £50,000 and sold them in March 2023 for £145,000. It had no other disposals in the CAP y/e 31/12/2023.

Cee Limited had a capital loss brought forward from the previous CAP of £25,000. The indexation factor from August 1998 to December 2017 is 0.729.

Calculate the chargeable gain that will form part of the taxable total profits for Cee Limited for the CAP.

4.4   Aye Limited made the following disposal in March 2023. This was its only disposal during CAP y/e 31/12/2023.

It sold a factory for £500,000 that had been used since it was bought new for £300,000 in September 1986.

Required:

Calculate the chargeable gains arising from the disposal. The relevant indexation factor is:

September 1986 to December 2017   1.829

4.5   Dee Limited made the following disposal in its CAP y/e 31/12/2023.

It sold 10,000 of its ordinary shares in Zydeco Ltd on 30/03/2023 for £60,000 in total. The shareholding in this company had been built up as follows:

1/1/1992   Bought 3,000 shares for £3.00 each

1/1/1995   Bought 12,000 shares for £3.50 each

1 /1/1999   Received bonus shares on the basis of 1 for 5

1 /1/2000   Sold 5,000 shares

Required:

•   Calculate any chargeable gain made on:

       – the disposal of shares in March 2023

The relevant indexation factors are:

January 1992 to January 1995   0.077

January 1995 to January 2000   0.141

January 2000 to December 2017   0.669

4.6 Practice Ltd bought 5,000 shares in Luncheon Ltd for £15,500 in October 2001. A rights issue of 1 for 50 shares was bought in July 2003 for £2 per share. In April 2023, Practice Ltd sold all the shares for £9 per share.

Indexation factors are: October 2001 to July 2003: 0.114; July 2003 to December 2017: 0.534

What is the gain made on these shares?

	No. Shares	Cost £	Indexed cost £

Proceeds	£
Indexed Cost	£
Gain	£

4.7 Exe Ltd purchased a factory in April 2006 for £720,000. The company purchased a warehouse in January 2024 for £1,150,000.

The factory was sold in March 2024 for £1,270,000.

The indexation factor from April 2006 to December 2017 is 0.415

Calculate the chargeable gain on the sale of the factory, after any rollover relief.

5 Corporation Tax – calculating the tax

this chapter covers...

In this chapter we bring together all the results of our studies of Corporation Tax in Chapters 1 to 4, and learn how to calculate the Corporation Tax itself. To do this we start by reviewing the components of the computation, including an examination of deductions for qualifying charitable donations.

We then go on to study how Corporation Tax is calculated.

We will then review the process and options for offsetting various losses, and consider the issues that can affect the choice of optimum loss set off. We will also review the division of profits from all sources when dealing with an accounting period of over 12 months.

The chapter is completed with sections on interest and penalties and record keeping.

THE CORPORATION TAX COMPUTATION

structure of the computation

As discussed in earlier chapters, the Corporation Tax computation starts with a summary of profits from various sources that are chargeable to Corporation Tax. The computation then goes on to calculate the amount of Corporation Tax that is payable.

A separate computation will need to be carried out for each Chargeable Accounting Period (CAP), which will result in a tax liability for the period. A separate CT600 return form will also need to be completed for each CAP. A simple version of this computation is repeated here:

Trading Income		X
+	Profits from Investments	X
+	Chargeable Gains	X
=	Taxable Total Profits	X
	Corporation Tax on taxable total profits	X

Note that 'taxable total profits' were previously known as 'profits chargeable to Corporation Tax' (PCTCT).

revision – what we have covered so far

In Chapters 2 and 3 we examined in detail how the 'Trading Income' figure is calculated, including the calculation of capital allowances for plant and machinery and for structures and buildings. In Chapter 4 we saw how chargeable gains are calculated on individual chargeable disposals and combined ready for inclusion in the Corporation Tax computation.

where we go from here

In this chapter we will be looking at the final stage of the Corporation Tax computation – bringing all the income together and working out the Corporation Tax liability. Finally we will look briefly at the sort of records that should be kept to show how the figures in the computation have been arrived at, and various penalties.

You may recall the summary diagram from Chapter 2, reproduced at the top of the next page. We have now looked in detail at the elements in the first three of the boxes along the top of the diagram, and will now follow the rest of the procedures over the next few pages.

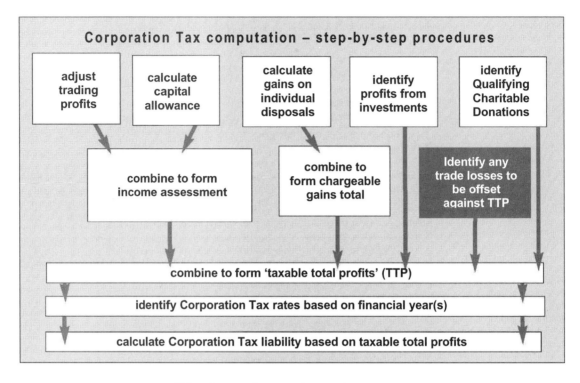

profits from investments

You will see from the above diagram that profits from investments need to be identified so that they can be incorporated into the computation. These profits could include:

■ **interest received from non-trade investments**

The gross amount of any interest receivable (ie on an **accruals basis**) during the CAP forms an investment income assessment that is brought into the main computation. Examples of the sources of interest include bank and building society deposits, debentures and Government securities ('gilts'). You can assume that any such interest in an examination task is non-trade, and should therefore be treated in this way. This interest is the main part of what is often referred to as a 'non-trade loan relationship' (NTLR).

■ **profits from renting out property**

The tax-adjusted profits from rental income are assessed as 'property income' on an accruals basis. You would not be expected to carry out complex adjustments to such figures, and would just need to incorporate the profit figure into the main computation. A little later in this chapter we will see how to deal with any losses that may arise from this type of income.

You should note that **dividends received** from other UK companies are not brought into the Corporation Tax computation, and are not taxed. This is because the profits from which they derive have already been taxed through the other company's computation.

'qualifying charitable donations' (QCD)

Companies are entitled to make gifts to charities under this scheme, and obtain tax relief on their payments. This operates simply by allowing the company to deduct the amount of the payment from the total profits in the Corporation Tax computation. This is known as a 'charge', and carried out as the final stage in the calculation of the taxable total profits. The **payment date determines which CAP** the QCD falls into – for example, if the payment was made during a 'long' accounting period. Unlike the gift-aid scheme for individuals (that you may have come across in 'personal tax'), the company makes the payment to the charity as a gross amount, with no adjustment for tax. As we saw in Chapter 2, the company cannot use a QCD as an allowable deduction in the calculation of Trading Income profits, since this would form a duplication of tax relief.

If there are insufficient total profits to set a QCD against in the final calculation of taxable total profits, then the tax relief on the balance of the payment is lost, since it cannot be carried forward. Where trading losses are set against the taxable total profits (as outlined in Chapter 2), this is carried out in priority to QCDs, so again there is a possibility of losing the tax relief on the charitable donation.

We will now use a Case Study to demonstrate how the various elements are combined into a Corporation Tax computation, before looking at the tax calculation itself.

Case Study

THE BASIC COMPANY LIMITED: CALCULATING THE TTP

The Basic Company Limited (which has no associated companies) has produced accounts for the year ended 31/3/2024. The accounts have been adjusted for tax purposes, and the following figures have been established:

	£
Adjusted Trading Profit (before capital allowances)	1,000,000
Capital Allowances – Plant & Machinery	163,000
Payment to Charity under QCD scheme	28,000

	£
Non-Trade Interest Receivable	55,000
Dividends Received from UK Company	90,000
Chargeable Gains	34,000
Rental Income	48,000

required

Using a Corporation Tax Computation, calculate the taxable total profits for the CAP y/e 31/3/2024.

solution

In order to complete the computation, the trading income assessment must first be established:

	£
Adjusted Trading Profits	1,000,000
less Plant & Machinery capital allowances	(163,000)
Trading Income assessment	837,000

Building on the outline computation shown at the start of this chapter, we can now combine the figures that make up the taxable total profits.

Corporation Tax Computation

	£
Trading Income	837,000
Profits from Investments:	
Non-Trade Interest Receivable	55,000
Property Income	48,000
Chargeable Gains	34,000
	974,000
less Qualifying Charitable Donations	(28,000)
Taxable total profits	946,000

Note the structure of the computation, since you will need to use this without further guidance. Note also that the dividends received of £90,000 are left out of the calculation entirely.

In the next section we will see how the tax itself is calculated.

CALCULATING THE CORPORATION TAX LIABILITY

The rates for Corporation Tax depend on the Financial Year that the CAP falls into, and for Financial Year 2023 it also depends on the level of taxable total profits (TTP). The following table shows the rates.

Taxable Total Profits (TTP)	Financial Year 2022 (ie 1/4/2022 – 31/3/2023)	Financial Year 2023 (ie 1/4/2023 – 31/3/2024)
£0 - £50,000		Small profits rate 19%
£50,001 - £250,000	Main rate 19%	Main rate 25% less marginal relief
Over £250,000		Main rate 25%

As can be seen, all levels of profits for CAPs that fall entirely into Financial Year 2022 (or, in fact, into recent earlier financial years) are taxed at the main rate of 19%. For CAPs that fall entirely into Financial Year 2023, the level of taxable total profits determines the Corporation Tax rate and calculation.

The levels of taxable total profits of £50,000 and £250,000 shown in the table relate to

■ A 12 month CAP, and

■ A company that does not have any associated companies (ie is not part of a group of companies).

We can use the data from the previous case study to see what rate of tax applies and calculate the Corporation Tax for The Basic Company Limited. The company has a 12 month CAP falling entirely in FY 2023, and it has no associated companies.

The rate of Corporation Tax that will apply to this CAP is the main rate of 25% because the taxable total profits (of £946,000) are above £250,000.

The Corporation Tax liability for the Basic Company Limited for the CAP ending 31/3/2024 is

£946,000 x 25% = £236,500

adjusting limits

Where the CAP (or relevant part of the CAP) is shorter than 12 months, then the limits applied will be reduced by time apportionment. For example, a 6 month CAP falling into FY 2023 would use limits of £25,000 and £125,000 (ie 6/12 of the normal limits) to determine the rate of tax.

Where a company has one or more associated companies, then the limits applied would be divided by the number of associated companies plus one. For example, a company with a 12 month CAP in FY 2023 that had 3 associated companies (ie in a group of 4 companies) would use limits divided by 4 to give limits of £50,000 / 4 = £12,500 and £250,000 / 4 = £62,500.

Where a company has both a short CAP, and associated companies, then both reductions would apply. For example, a company with a 9 month CAP in FY 2023 and one associated company would apply limits of £50,000 x 9/12 x ½ = £18,750 and £250,000 x 9/12 x ½ = £93,750 to determine the tax rate.

marginal relief

You will see from the table that marginal relief applies to situations that fall between the two limits of £50,000 and £250,000 for a 12 month CAP in FY 2023 for a company with no associated companies.

Marginal relief is calculated as

$$3/200 \text{ x (upper limit – TTP)}$$

Marginal relief is then deducted from Corporation Tax calculated at the main rate of 25% to arrive at the final amount of tax.

For example, a company with a 12 month CAP ending on 31/3/2024, with no associated companies and taxable total profits of £180,000, would have a Corporation Tax calculation as follows:

	£
£180,000 x 25% (main rate)	45,000
less marginal relief:	
3/200 x (£250,000 – £180,000)	(1,050)
Corporation Tax	43,950

where CAPs straddle 1/4/2023

Where a CAP straddles 1/4/2023 and falls into both financial years, then the profits must be time-apportioned and the appropriate calculations applied to each part to arrive at the total tax for the CAP. The limits that are applied to the part of the CAP that is in Financial Year 2023 will be reduced to take account of the length of that part of the CAP.

For example, a company with a 12 month CAP ending on 31/12/2023, with no associated companies and taxable total profits of £320,000 would be dealt with as follows:

The part of the CAP that falls into Financial Year 2022 is 3 months (1/1/23 to 31/3/23), and therefore the time-apportioned profits relating to that period are £320,000 x 3/12 = £80,000. Since the Corporation Tax rate in FY 2022 is 19% for all levels of profit, the Corporation Tax for this part of the CAP is

£80,000 x 19% £15,200

The part of the CAP that falls into the Financial Year 2023 is 9 months (1/4/23 to 31/12/23), and the time-apportioned profits are £320,000 x 9/12 = £240,000. The upper limit which is applied in this part of the CAP is £250,000 x 9/12 = £187,500. The Corporation Tax rate that is applied for this part of the CAP is therefore the main rate of 25%, since the profits exceed the upper limit. The Corporation Tax for this part of the CAP is

£240,000 x 25% £60,000

The total Corporation Tax for the CAP is £15,200 + £60,000 = £75,200.

We will now use a case study to illustrate the calculation of Corporation Tax in various situations.

Case Study

THE COMPLEX PRACTICE
CORPORATION TAX CALCULATIONS

The Complex Practice has various unconnected clients, and you have been asked to calculate the Corporation Tax liability for each client, based on the following details.

Aye Limited has a 12 month CAP ending on 31/3/2024. It has no associated companies, and taxable total profits of £200,000.

Bee Limited has an 8 month CAP ending on 31/12/2023. It has no associated companies, and taxable total profits of £180,000.

Cee Limited has a 12 month CAP ending on 31/3/2024. It has one associated company, and taxable total profits of £120,000.

Dee Limited has a 12 month CAP ending on 30/9/2023. It has no associated companies, and taxable total profits of £46,000.

required

Calculate the Corporation Tax liability for each client.

solution

Aye Limited

The taxable total profits of £200,000 fall between the limits of £50,000 and £250,000, so the company will pay tax at main rate less marginal relief.

	£
£200,000 x 25% (main rate)	50,000
less marginal relief:	
3/200 x (£250,000 - £200,000)	(750)
Corporation Tax	49,250

Bee Limited

The CAP is 8 months, so the relevant limits will be £50,000 x 8/12 = £33,333 and £250,000 x 8/12 = £166,666. The taxable total profits of £180,000 exceed the upper limit, so the company will pay Corporation Tax at the main rate.

£180,000 x 25%	£45,000

Cee Limited

This company has one associated company, so the normal 12 month limits will be divided by 2, to give £25,000 and £125,000. The taxable total profits of £120,000 fall between these limits, so the company will pay Corporation Tax at main rate minus marginal relief.

	£
£120,000 x 25% (main rate)	30,000
less marginal relief:	
3/200 x (£125,000 - £120,000)	(75)
Corporation Tax	29,925

Dee Limited

This company has a CAP which straddles 1/4/2023, with 6 months (£23,000 taxable total profits) in each financial year.

The part of the CAP that falls into FY 2022 will be taxed at the main rate of 19%, since limits are not applicable in this financial year.

£23,000 x 19%	£4,370

The part of the CAP that falls into FY 2023 will use limits of 6/12 of the full limits to give £25,000 and £125,000. The profits of £23,000 fall below the lower limit, so the profits will be taxed at the small profits rate of 19%.

£23,000 x 19%	£4,370

The total Corporation Tax for the CAP is £4,370 + £4,370 = £8,740.

DEALING WITH A VARIETY OF LOSSES

Over the last few chapters we have seen how different sorts of losses can be relieved against profits.

- in Chapter 2 we saw that recent trading losses for an ongoing business can be:
  - carried forward against future taxable total profits before QCD payments, or
  - set against the current period taxable total profits before QCD payments, and if this has been done,
  - then set against the taxable total profits before QCD payments of the previous twelve months

- in Chapter 4 we saw that capital losses on a disposal are first set against chargeable gains arising in the same CAP, and then carried forward against chargeable gains in the future

- rental losses can be set against the current period taxable total profits and any amount not used carried forward and set against future taxable total profits before QCD payments

We must therefore be careful if presented with a variety of losses to deal with each one correctly. Although the above rules are fairly straightforward, they must be learnt, since it would be easy to get confused.

We will use a Case Study now to illustrate how to deal with a variety of losses.

Case Study

LOSER PLC:
DEALING WITH DIFFERENT LOSSES

Loser plc has the following adjusted results for the CAPs y/e 31/3/2023, and y/e 31/3/2024.

	CAP y/e 31/3/2023	CAP y/e 31/3/2024
	£	£
Trading Profit / (Loss)	(300,000)	500,000
Rental Profit / (Loss)	(15,000)	45,000
Non-Trade Interest Receivable	425,000	210,000
Chargeable Gains / (Capital Loss)	(50,000)	120,000

The company has not received dividends from other UK companies. The company did not make any Qualifying Charitable Donations.

required

1   Explain how the rental losses and capital losses must be offset, and describe the alternative ways in which the trading loss could be offset.

2   Calculate the Corporation Tax liability for the CAPs y/e 31/3/2023 and y/e 31/3/2024, based on each alternative.

3   Recommend how the trading loss should be offset, and explain your reasoning.

solution

1   The rental loss of £15,000 is set against the taxable total profits for the year ended 31/3/2023, giving a net figure of £410,000. The capital loss must be carried forward to the next CAP, to reduce the Chargeable Gains amount. This will give a chargeable gains assessment of £120,000 − £50,000 = £70,000 in the CAP to 31/3/2024.

The trading loss could either be:

(a) set against the taxable total profits of the CAP y/e 31/3/2023; since the only profits in that period are from interest receivable less the rental loss, the trade loss would reduce the taxable total profits of the CAP to £410,000 − £300,000 = £110,000. In this situation there is no opportunity to carry the loss back to the year before, since there is sufficient taxable total profits in the y/e 31/3/2023 to utilise all the loss

(b) carried forward and set against the taxable total profits of the CAP y/e 31/3/2024 (or a later CAP); this would reduce the taxable total profits amount for that period to £825,000 − £300,000 = £525,000

2   The tax computations are as follows:

Option (a)

	CAP y/e 31/3/2023 £	CAP y/e 31/3/2024 £
Trading Income	0	500,000
Property Income	0	45,000
Interest Receivable	425,000	210,000
Chargeable Gains	0	70,000
less Loss on Property Income	(15,000)	–
less Trading Loss of the year	(300,000)	–
Taxable total profits	110,000	825,000
Corporation Tax	(1) 20,900	(2) 206,250

Corporation Tax Workings:

	£
(1) Taxed at main rate:	
£110,000 × 19% =	20,900

(2)   Taxed at main rate:

£825,000 × 25% =   206,250

Option (b)

	CAP y/e 31/3/2023	CAP y/e 31/3/2024
	£	£
Trading Income	0	500,000
Property Income	0	45,000
Interest Receivable	425,000	210,000
Chargeable Gains	0	70,000
less Loss on Property Income	(15,000)	–
less trading loss bf	–	(300,000)
Taxable total profits	410,000	525,000
Corporation Tax	(1) 77,900	(2) 131,250

Corporation Tax Workings:

(1)   Taxed at main rate:

£410,000 × 19% =   77,900

(2)   Taxed at main rate:

£525,000 × 25% =   131,250

3   In this situation the total amount of Corporation Tax for the two CAPs is different in each option due to the change in tax rates.

Option (a)   £20,900 + £206,250 = £227,150

Option (b)   £77,900 + £131,250 = £209,150

Option (b) incurs total Corporation Tax over the two CAPs £18,000 less than option (a), and therefore option (b) should be chosen. The only disadvantage of this choice is that more of the total tax is paid earlier (relating to the first CAP) – a cash flow disadvantage.

SPLITTING ALL PROFITS FOR LONG ACCOUNTING PERIODS

In Chapter 2 we learned how to deal with the split of trading profits when a long period of account needs to be divided into two Chargeable Accounting Periods. Now that we have also looked at the other components of taxable total profits, it is a good time to review this technique and see how other profits are split.

trading profits (before deducting capital allowances)

As discussed earlier, the trading profits for the whole long period are adjusted, and the resulting adjusted trading profit is then time-apportioned.

capital allowances

Separate capital allowance computations are carried out for each CAP. The capital allowances are then deducted from the time-apportioned trading profits that were described above.

interest from non-trade investments

This income is calculated on an accruals basis, and is split based on how much relates to each period (the amount arising).

profits from renting out property

The profits from renting out property are also calculated on an accruals basis. These are split based on how much relates to each period (the amount arising).

chargeable gains

Chargeable gains are allocated to each period based on when each disposal takes place.

taxable total profits

The taxable total profits for each CAP are calculated by adding together the above elements. Any qualifying charitable donations (QCDs) are deducted from the relevant figure based on the date of payment.

INTEREST AND PENALTIES

interest

Where tax is paid after the due date (or a lower amount is paid than is due), interest is charged. This applies both to large companies that need to pay by instalments, and other companies that should pay nine months and one day after the end of the CAP. The interest rates are laid down by HM Revenue & Customs.

If a company overpays its Corporation Tax (or pays early), interest is payable to the company (although the interest rates are generally lower than amounts charged on overdue tax). Interest that is paid to the company is taxable, but interest payable is an allowable deduction against non-trading interest.

penalties for not telling HMRC your company is liable for Corporation Tax

HMRC must be made aware that the company is liable to pay tax (for example, if the company has just started trading). This must be done within three months of the start of business activities. This is usually done on a 'new company details' form. It is also known as 'chargeability to tax'.

If HMRC is not informed, then a penalty can arise. The penalty will be based on a percentage of the 'potential lost revenue' which is the Corporation Tax that would be due. The penalty ranges from 0% (if 'reasonable care was taken') to 100% (if the act was deliberate and concealed) of the potential lost revenue.

This is the same system that applies to errors in tax returns and is explained on the next page.

late return penalties

There are also penalties for failure to submit a Corporation Tax Return on time. These are divided into flat amount and percentage penalties:

- the initial penalties are £100 for submitting up to three months late and £200 for submitting more than three months late. These can increase for repeated occurrences

- in addition, 10% of the Corporation Tax relating to the return period can be charged where the return is 6-12 months late, increasing to 20% for over 12 months

penalties system for errors in tax returns and documents

A company can amend a return that it has submitted up to 12 months after the filing date. A system for penalties applies for incorrect information stated in tax returns and documents. This is based on a percentage of the extra tax due, depending on the behaviour that gave rise to the error. If the error is:

- due to **lack of reasonable care**, the penalty will be between 0% and 30% of the extra tax due

- **deliberate**, the penalty will be between 20% and 70% of the extra tax due, and if

- **deliberate and concealed**, the penalty will be between 30% and 100% of the extra tax due

The penalty also depends on whether the disclosure was prompted or unprompted. This gives the following series of penalty rates:

Type of behaviour	Unprompted disclosure	Prompted disclosure
Reasonable care	No penalty	No penalty
Careless	0% to 30%	15% to 30%
Deliberate	20% to 70%	35% to 70%
Deliberate and concealed	30% to 100%	50% to 100%

The percentage can be reduced if the taxpayer or their agent tells HMRC about the error(s), helps them work out the extra tax, and gives HMRC access to check the figures.

If the taxpayer made an error despite taking 'reasonable care' then no penalty will arise.

This system also applies to Income Tax.

failure to keep records

There can be a penalty for not keeping the required records for the correct length of time of up to £3,000 per Chargeable Accounting Period for companies.

HMRC enquiries

HMRC may open an 'enquiry' into a company's tax return, either at random, or because they believe that income and/or expenses may be misstated. The company must be notified about an enquiry within 12 months of the submission of the tax return.

The enquiry can lead to requests for documents to be produced to HMRC. There is an initial penalty for failure to supply the requested documents of £300 plus £60 per day that the failure continues.

The company may amend their return within 12 months of the filing date (as noted earlier), but any change in the amount of tax due will not take effect until any enquiry is completed.

On completion of an enquiry, HMRC will issue a closure notice and make any necessary amendments to the tax due. The company has 30 days to appeal this decision.

Where there has been an enquiry into a business where there is complexity, avoidance or large amounts of tax at risk, a part of the enquiry can be closed while the rest remains open. This is done by the issue by HMRC of a 'Partial Closure Notice' (PCN). This will provide greater certainty about the tax owed on individual discrete matters.

KEEPING RECORDS

general principles

Accounting records must be retained by a business, including a company, or its agent (for example, an accountant) for at least six years after the end of the accounting period. This period is extended if an enquiry is taking place.

A business will normally archive appropriate accounting records automatically for six years to satisfy the requirements of a variety of statutes, including the Companies Acts and the Limitation Act (which allows legal action to be brought on a contract for up to six years after a breach of that contract). Documents such as invoices, for example, are evidence of contracts of sale.

These records will need to be made available for a number of interested parties – and particularly in the unfortunate event of an inspection or investigation being made:

- auditors (when an audit is required)
- HM Revenue & Customs for both Corporation taxes and VAT
- Department of Work & Pensions

Typical records include:

- ledger accounts and daybooks – manual or computerised
- financial documents, eg invoices, credit notes, bank statements, cheque book stubs
- payroll records
- VAT records

records relating to tax computations

A company will need to keep for at least six years from the end of the accounting period, as part of the general archiving process, a number of records which specifically relate to Corporation Tax matters. These include:

- statements of profit or loss (income statements) and statements of financial position (balance sheets)
- taxation working papers, including capital allowance computations
- copies of tax returns
- invoices relating to allowable expenses and the acquisition of non-current (fixed) assets
- details of non-trade income
- non-current asset schedules

time limits for assessments and claims

Where a company discovers an error in a previous year's tax return and wants to adjust the return (perhaps to claim a tax repayment) the time limit is four years from the end of the tax year.

The same four year limit applies to HMRC when they discover errors in returns (as discussed earlier), provided the company has taken reasonable care. If the errors are the result of careless behaviour by the company, the time limit is six years, and if the behaviour was deliberate, the time limit is twenty years.

<table>
<tr>
<td>

Chapter Summary

</td>
<td>

▓ The Corporation Tax computation for a Chargeable Accounting Period (CAP) involves combining profits from various sources, and deducting any qualifying donations made to charity.

▓ A single rate of Corporation Tax applies to the taxable total profits (TTP) in FY2022, but a more complex system in FY2023.

▓ Property income losses are initially set against the taxable total profits of the current period, with any remaining balance carried forward to be set against the first available taxable total profit. Capital losses can only be carried forward to offset against capital gains. There are various options for dealing with trade losses.

▓ Corporation Tax is payable a maximum of nine months and one day after the end of the CAP. For 'large' companies, instalments may need to be paid, based on the estimated tax payable.

▓ The company tax return (CT600) is due to be submitted twelve months after the end of the accounting period.

▓ Appropriate records must be kept for at least six years from the end of the accounting period.

</td>
</tr>
</table>

<table>
<tr>
<td>

Key Terms

</td>
<td>

taxable total profits (TTP)

</td>
<td>

this is the figure used as the basis for calculation of Corporation Tax for a limited company. It includes trading income, profits from investments, and chargeable gains, and is charged after QCD payments have been deducted. It is calculated for each Chargeable Accounting Period (CAP) within which the company operates

</td>
</tr>
<tr>
<td></td>
<td>

chargeable accounting period (CAP)

</td>
<td>

this is the period for which the TTP must be calculated. It is the same as the period for which the company produces financial accounts, unless that period is for more than twelve months. In that case the financial accounting period is divided into two CAPs

</td>
</tr>
<tr>
<td></td>
<td>

qualifying charitable donations (QCD)

</td>
<td>

a system which allows payments that companies have made to charity to be deducted in the final calculation of taxable total profits. This provides the company with tax relief on the payment and is known as a 'charge'

</td>
</tr>
<tr>
<td></td>
<td>

CT600

</td>
<td>

the self-assessment Corporation Tax return for limited companies. One form must be completed for each CAP

</td>
</tr>
</table>

Activities

5.1 The Management Company Limited (that has no associated companies) has produced accounts for the year ended 31/3/24. The accounts have been adjusted for tax purposes, and the following figures have been established.

	£
Adjusted Trading Profit (before capital allowances)	1,120,000
Capital Allowances – Plant & Machinery	63,000
Payment to Charity under QCD scheme	45,000
Non-Trade Interest Receivable	60,000
Dividends Received from UK Company	90,000
Chargeable Gains	48,000
Rental Income	23,000

Required:

Using a Corporation Tax Computation, calculate the taxable total profits for the CAP, and the Corporation Tax payable.

Carry out all calculations to the nearest £.

5.2 The Resource Company Limited has produced accounts for the year ended 31/3/24. The accounts have been adjusted for tax purposes, and the following figures have been established. The company has three associated companies.

	£
Adjusted Trading Profit (before capital allowances)	1,420,000
Capital Allowances – Plant & Machinery	205,000
Payment to Charity under QCD scheme	8,000
Non-Trade Interest Receivable	12,000
Dividends Received from UK Company	27,000
Chargeable Gains	88,000
Capital Loss brought forward from previous year	18,000
Rental Income	92,000

Required:

Using a Corporation Tax Computation, calculate the taxable total profits for the CAP, and the Corporation Tax payable.

Carry out all calculations to the nearest £.

5.3 The Quick Company Limited (that has no associated companies) has the following tax-adjusted results for the CAP y/e 31/12/23.

	£
Trading Loss	120,000
Chargeable Gains	90,000
Non-trade Interest Receivable	40,000
Rental Income	35,000
QCD Payment	10,000

The company also has capital losses brought forward of £8,000, and rental losses brought forward of £13,000.

The company wishes to obtain any relief for the offset of its trading loss as quickly as possible, and will therefore set it against the TTP of the current CAP.

Required:

Using a Corporation Tax Computation, calculate the taxable total profits for the CAP, and the Corporation Tax payable.

Carry out all calculations to the nearest £.

State an alternative option that may be available to this company for offsetting its trading loss.

5.4 Trade Trader Ltd (that has no associated companies) has an unadjusted income statement for the year ended 31/3/2024 as follows:

	£	£
Sales		720,000
less cost of sales		400,000
Gross profit		320,000
Interest receivable		50,000
Profit on disposal of non-current assets		50,000
Rental income receivable		40,000
		460,000
less expenses:		
Discounts allowed	11,000	
Salaries and wages	70,000	
Depreciation	41,000	
Bad debts written off	12,000	
Rates and insurance	13,000	
Postage and stationery	10,000	
Administration expenses	14,000	
Advertising	18,000	
Travel and entertaining	20,000	
		209,000
Net Profit		251,000

Notes:

- Administration includes £1,000 directors' speeding fines incurred while on company business.

- Advertising consists of:

    – gifts of mugs with company logos to 1000 customers totalled £8,000

    – gifts of food hampers with company logos to 400 other customers totalled £10,000

- Travel and entertaining is made up as follows:

	£
Employees' travel expenses	7,400
Employees' subsistence allowances	3,600
Entertaining customers	6,000
Entertaining staff on company trip to theme park	3,000
	20,000

The interest receivable is non-trade.

The profit on sale of non-current assets resulted in a chargeable gain of £41,000.

The rental income is assessable as Property Income, and the figure in the accounts can be used for tax purposes.

Capital allowances for the period have been calculated at £11,000.

Required:

1   Adjust the net profit shown to arrive at the trading income assessment for Corporation Tax purposes.

2   Calculate the taxable total profits.

3   Calculate the Corporation Tax payable.

Carry out all calculations to the nearest £.

5.5 Mastermind Limited is changing its accounting dates, and to accommodate this has produced one long set of financial accounts, from 1/4/2022 to 31/7/2023. It has no associated companies.

Capital allowances have already been calculated for each of the two CAPs as follows:

CAP 1/4/2022 to 31/3/2023 £8,000

CAP 1/4/2023 to 31/7/2023 £2,500

The financial accounts for the 16 months to 31/7/2023 are as follows:

	£	£
Sales		293,000
less cost of sales		155,000
Gross profit		138,000
add		
bad debts recovered		3,100
discounts received		2,000
less expenses:		143,100
Salaries and wages	68,500	
Rent, rates, and insurance	9,200	
Depreciation etc.	10,000	
General expenses	15,630	
Interest payable	8,300	
Bad debts written off	12,400	
Selling expenses	15,000	
		139,030
Net Profit		4,070

The following information is also provided:

- depreciation etc is made up as follows:

  – Depreciation £45,000

  – Loss on sale of computer £19,500

  – Profit on sale of Building £54,500

- general expenses include debt recovery fees of £800

- selling expenses include:
  - Entertaining customers   £1,930
  - Gifts of diaries to customers   £600
    (£6 each, with company advert)

The profit on the sale of the building resulted in a chargeable gain of £45,000 on 1/6/2023.

There were no other chargeable gains in either CAP.

Required:

- Adjust the financial accounts for the 16-month period, before deduction of capital allowances.

- Time-apportion the adjusted profit figure into CAPs.

- Calculate the trading income assessment for each CAP.

- Calculate the taxable total profits for each CAP.

- Calculate the Corporation Tax payable in respect of each CAP.

Carry out all calculations to the nearest £.

5.6   Tick the appropriate box for each of the following statements:

		True	False
(a)	If a company is five months late in submitting their tax return, they will receive a fixed penalty of £200.		
(b)	Penalties for errors made by companies in their tax return vary from 20% to 100%.		
(c)	If a company fails to keep records for the appropriate period of time, they can be fined £3,000.		
(d)	A company with a period of account ending on 30 April 2023 must keep their records until 30 April 2029.		

6 Income Tax – trading profits

this chapter covers...

In this chapter we turn our attention to the trading profits of sole traders and partnerships – these are taxed under Income Tax. Some of the treatment of these profits is similar to those examined under Corporation Tax, but there are many important differences.

We start by learning about what is considered 'trading' and therefore comes under the rules that we are going to study. The factors that help determine that a business is being carried out are called the 'badges of trade'.

We then go on to examine the normal basis of assessment for trading income, and also learn about allowable and non-allowable expenditure for sole traders and partners and see where it differs from the situation for limited companies.

Finally we examine the calculation of capital allowances, and see the similarities and important differences compared with Corporation Tax.

INTRODUCTION TO BUSINESS TAXATION OF INDIVIDUALS

In this book so far we have provided an introduction to the taxes that apply to business in the UK, and looked in detail at the way that Corporation Tax is applied to various types of profits of limited companies.

In the remaining chapters of this book we are going to examine how the trading profits and gains of business are subject to Income Tax and Capital Gains Tax. This applies to organisations that have not been formed as limited companies, but are operated by individuals who are sole traders or partners.

The business activities of these individuals are not legally separate from their personal financial interests, and therefore they are subject to Income Tax and Capital Gains Tax on their income and gains from all sources. The Unit 'Personal Tax' (covered in Osborne Books' Personal Tax text) examines how Income Tax and Capital Gains Tax are calculated. In this book we will examine the impact of these taxes on individuals' **business** profits and gains.

WHAT IS TRADING?

In order to appreciate the way that Income Tax applies to those who operate a trade, we must first understand exactly what constitutes **trading** from a tax point of view. Nearly all of us buy and sell things from time to time (for example we may change our cars regularly), but we usually wouldn't think of ourselves as traders. It is important to distinguish between a trading and non-trading situation, since:

- trading carried out by an individual is assessable to Income Tax as 'Trading Income'
- non-trading activities may be subject to Capital Gains Tax, or may be outside the scope of all taxation

HM Revenue & Customs uses several tests known as 'the badges of trade' to help decide whether it believes an activity should be classed as trading. The result of each of these tests will provide evidence in one direction or the other, and the final decision will be judged on the overall weight of evidence. These tests are described below.

the badges of trade

- **profit motive**

  Where profit is clearly the driving force behind the activity, then this is a strong indicator that the activity may constitute trading.

- **subject matter of the activity**

  Where the items bought and sold are of no personal use to the individual then this is further evidence of trading, and this case is strengthened if the individual already works in a situation where such items are traded. Where, however, the items are used by the individual or can provide personal pleasure then this would be evidence that the activity is not trading.

- **length of ownership**
  Where items are sold shortly after acquisition then this is an indicator of trading. Where they are held for a long period it may provide evidence that it is not trading.

- **frequency of transactions**
  Where there is a series of similar transactions, then this indicates trading. A single transaction is less likely to be considered as trading.

- **supplementary work**
  Where the individual carries out work on the items (eg repairs) to make them more saleable, this is evidence of trading.

- **reasons for acquisition and sale**
  An intentional purchase and planned sale will provide evidence of trading. An item that was given to the individual, or one that was sold quickly to raise money to pay personal debts is less likely to constitute trading.

- **source of finance**
  Where money is borrowed on a short-term basis to fund the purchase, this may provide evidence of trading if the item needed to be sold to repay the loan.

These tests will also apply (as far as possible) when considering whether the provision of a service amounts to a business.

We will now illustrate the use of these indicators with a Case Study.

Case Study

DAN THE BANGER MAN: BADGES OF TRADE

Dan works as an Assistant Accountant, but in his spare time will often be found working on one of his cars in his garage. He usually owns a couple of cars at the same time – one to drive around in and one that he is repairing. He goes to a car auction about once every six weeks and buys a car that needs a little work, provided it is at a good price. After he has repaired the car he usually keeps it for a few weeks to use, before advertising it in his local paper and selling it, so that he can obtain the best price. Dan regards this activity as his hobby, and has not needed to borrow money to finance it.

r e q u i r e d

Using the badges of trade, identify:

- the points that indicate that Dan is trading
- the points that suggest non-trading

Explain what conclusion you would reach from the balance of evidence.

solution

The badges of trade can be interpreted as follows:

- **Profit motive**
  Dan seems to deliberately buy and sell at a profit. He buys only at auction, and sets his own selling price through his adverts. This indicates trading.

- **Subject matter**
  Dan gets personal use from the cars that he buys, and this could indicate that he is not trading. The fact that he is not employed in the car trade helps this argument.

- **Length of ownership**
  After repairing the cars, Dan only keeps them for a few weeks. Such a short time indicates trading.

- **Frequency of transactions**
  The buying and selling of cars seems to be a regular activity, with purchases being made about every six weeks. This indicates trading.

- **Supplementary work**
  Repairing the cars counts as supplementary work, and Dan deliberately buys cars that need work carrying out. This indicates trading.

- **Reason for acquisition and sale**
  Acquisition appears to be planned with the ultimate sale in mind. This indicates trading.

- **Source of finance**
  Dan does not borrow money to finance his activity. However, it could be argued that the regular sale of cars provides the finance, just like in a normal trading situation.

In conclusion . . .

Overall, nearly all indicators point to trading. The only point that indicates the opposite is that Dan uses the cars before sale. The fact that he views his activity as a hobby is not relevant in the face of such evidence. It is likely that HM Revenue & Customs would wish to assess his income from this activity as Trading Income.

notification of starting trading

When an individual starts trading he/she must notify HM Revenue and Customs. This is known as 'notification of chargeability to tax'. The time limit is within six months of the end of the tax year for Income Tax and NIC purposes. HMRC will then arrange to tax the income as 'Trading Income' under the self-assessment system as described in the next section.

trading allowance

Where it has been established that an individual is trading (although on a small scale), a tax-free trading allowance of up to £1,000 may be available. This is an automatic deduction from gross trading income (ie sales) which is an alternative to normal allowable expenses. It can therefore eliminate taxable profits from gross trading income of up to £1,000.

Where gross trading income is over £1,000, the trading allowance can still be used instead of the normal allowable expenses if they are less than £1,000.

This will reduce the taxable amount.

Where gross trading income is less than £1,000, but allowable expenses are more than income, it will be beneficial to elect not to claim the trading allowance. In this way a loss can be established that can be offset using the rules that will be explained later.

The trading allowance is only available to individuals. It is not available to partnerships or limited companies. There is also an equivalent 'property allowance' that can be used by individuals who receive small amounts of rental income.

EMPLOYED OR SELF-EMPLOYED?

In these chapters we are mainly concerned with self-employed individuals or those in partnership. Before we look at these situations in detail we must ensure that we can distinguish between workers who are employed (and therefore pay Income Tax and National Insurance through PAYE) and those who are self-employed and invoice for their work and account for their own Income Tax and NIC.

The distinction is whether the contract that applies is one **of service** (when the person is an **employee**), or a contract **for services** (a **self-employed** relationship). These can be confusing phrases, but if you think a contract:

- **of service** could apply to a servant (where the employee serves the employer)
- **for services** could apply to someone who invoices 'for services rendered' and is self-employed

In some cases it can be difficult to establish whether the person is employed or self-employed, and HMRC has produced leaflets and an online 'Employment Status Indicator' tool to help.

The following are indicators that help provide evidence in one direction or the other.

Indicators of employment	Indicators of self-employment
Need to do the work yourself	Can employ helper or substitute
Told how, where and when to do work	Decide yourself how, when and where to do work
Work set hours and paid regular wage with sick pay and holidays	Choose work hours and invoice for work done
No risk of capital or losses	Risk own capital and bear losses from work that is not to standard
Employer provides equipment	Provide own equipment
Work for one employer (but sometimes more)	Work for several people or organisations

THE BASIS OF ASSESSMENT OF TRADING PROFITS

Trading profits (both for sole traders and those in partnership) and professional profits are assessed to Income Tax as 'Trading Income'.

The trading income assessment for a sole trader will form part of his/her income that is taxable under Income Tax, and will be incorporated into the personal Income Tax computation. We examined this briefly in Chapter 1, and you may also have studied it in the 'personal tax' Unit.

The assessable trading profits of a partnership are divided between the partners according to the partnership agreement, and each partner's share then forms part of their individual Income Tax computation.

basis of assessment

Sole traders and partnerships can produce their annual accounts up to any date in the year that they choose. Once the business is established, most accounting years will consistently follow the same pattern.

The basis of assessment for trading income of sole traders and partners is the adjusted profit arising in the tax year (6th April to following 5th April). This is a change from the previous 'current year' basis, which is outside your area of study. If accounts are produced exactly in line with the tax year, or up to 31 March each year, then they will be adjusted for tax purposes, as we will examine shortly, and form the assessable trading income.

If accounts are produced up to any other date in the year, then apportionment will need to be carried out after the figures have been adjusted for tax purposes, to provide figures for the tax year. This apportionment is outside your area of study, and so are the transitional arrangements that will apply to existing businesses that previously used the old 'current year basis'.

The term 'adjusted profits' refers to profits (on an accruals basis) that have been adjusted for tax purposes, and incorporate any capital allowances. This procedure is very similar to the one that we studied in Chapters 2 and 3 in connection with Corporation Tax for limited companies.

ADJUSTING THE TRADING PROFITS OF AN ACCOUNTING PERIOD

The procedure for adjusting profits for sole traders and partnerships is very similar to the one used for companies in Chapter 2. This means that you can use a lot of the knowledge gained in that area and apply it to this situation. We will firstly review the way that the procedure works, and then identify the main differences that you will encounter when dealing with trading under Income Tax rules in comparison with Corporation Tax.

review of adjusting profits

The object of adjusting the financial accounts is to make sure that:

- the only income that is credited is trading income
- the only expenditure that is deducted is allowable trading expenditure

When we adjust profits, we will start with the profit from the financial accounts, and:

- deduct any income that is not trading income, and
- add back any expenditure that has already been deducted but is not allowable

adjusting income

Provided that the 'sales' amount relates entirely to trading, this figure will not need adjusting. Other income may or may not be taxable, but if it does not fall under trading income, then it will need to be adjusted for in the trading profit calculation. The following examples of non-trading income that were given in Chapter 2 are also valid in this situation:

- non-trading interest receivable
- rent receivable
- gains on the disposal of non-current (fixed) assets
- dividends received

adjusting expenditure

We will only need to adjust for any expenditure accounted for in the financial accounts profit if it is not allowable. We do this by adding it back to the financial accounts profit. Expenditure that is allowable can be left unadjusted in the accounts.

The general rule for expenditure to be allowable in a trading income computation is that it must be:

- revenue rather than capital in nature, and
- 'wholly and exclusively' for the purpose of the trade

The rules that we examined in Chapter 2 regarding whether repair costs are capital or revenue also apply here.

Expenditure that has a 'dual purpose' is therefore strictly speaking not allowable in its entirety (for example, travel expenses for a trip combining a business conference and a holiday). However, expenditure that can be divided into a part that was wholly business and a part that is wholly private could be apportioned and have the business portion allowed. This could apply to motoring expenses.

Members of the sole trader's or partner's family are sometimes employed in their business – for example, spouses or children. This will be an allowable expense provided the amount paid is reasonable for the work carried out. For example, paying a son or daughter £40,000 per year for occasional help in the office would not be an allowable deduction (but £5,000 may be). If a relative is employed then PAYE would need to be applied to their earnings in the normal way.

adjusting accounts of companies and individuals

■ **issues not arising for sole traders and partnerships**

The following items will not appear in the accounts that we will be adjusting for Income Tax purposes:

– dividends payable

– Corporation Tax

– payments to directors

■ **issues arising only for sole traders and partnerships**

– private expenditure of the owner(s) – this is non-allowable expenditure.

This could arise where entirely private expenditure had been paid through the business accounts (eg a personal electricity bill), or where certain expenditure needs to be apportioned between business and personal use. This latter situation is possible for expenditure such as motor expenses where business and private mileage could be used to apportion the total cost. As we will see later, there is a similar adjustment that is made to capital allowances on items with some private use.

– drawings of the owner(s) – these are not allowable deductions.

If the accounts have been produced following normal good accounting practice, then drawings will not appear before the net profit figure, and therefore no adjustment will be necessary. However, some accounts may have been prepared to include drawing in the profit calculation, possibly under the heading of 'wages' and here the figure must be added back in the adjustment.

– taking trading goods out of the business for private use – this is also non-allowable, but requires particular care.

In contrast to normal accounting practice, these goods need to be accounted for tax purposes at their normal selling price. This means that any profit that would have been made by selling the goods normally through the business is still assessable. If there is no other specific information to guide you, the normal mark-up profit percentage (from the accounts) should be added to the cost price when adjusting the accounts.

We will now summarise some common expenditure items that are allowable and non-allowable in the form of a table. We will then illustrate the points by means of a Case Study.

Allowable expenditure	Non-allowable expenditure
Revenue expenditure wholly and exclusively for trade	Capital expenditure and private revenue expenditure
Cost of sales	Goods for private use
Staff salaries & wages (including relatives if amount paid is in line with work carried out) (including employers' NIC)	Drawings of owner(s) (including self-employed NIC, pension payments and Income Tax); excessive payments for employing relatives
Entertaining staff	Entertaining customers or suppliers
Certain gifts to customers (up to £50 each p.a., not food, drink, tobacco or vouchers)	All other gifts to customers
Trade bad debts written off	Non-trade bad debts written off
Increases in specific bad debt provisions	Increases in general bad debt provisions
Staff fines for minor motoring offences (eg parking)	All other fines for lawbreaking (owners and staff)
Donations to local charities	Donations to political parties and to national charities
Capital allowances	Depreciation

Case Study

THE SOLE TRADER: ADJUSTING TRADING PROFITS

Rachel Sole is a fishmonger, operating under the trade name of 'The Sole Trader'.

Her draft accounts for the year are as follows:

	£	£
Sales		64,000
less cost of sales:		
Opening inventory (stock)	6,000	
Purchases	30,000	
	36,000	
less closing inventory (stock)	4,000	
		32,000
Gross profit		32,000
add: building society interest rec'd		600
		32,600
less expenses:		
Rent, Rates & Insurance	1,500	
Part-Time Employee's Wages	5,500	
Employers' NIC for Part Time Employee	112	
Depreciation on Fittings	1,250	
Increase in General Provision for Bad Debts	550	
General Expenses	1,450	
Purchase of new Freezer Cabinet	1,000	
Wages drawn for self	15,100	
Personal pension contribution for self	400	
		26,862
Net Profit		5,738

Notes:

1   Rachel pays the combined electricity bill for the shop and her private flat out of her personal bank account. The amount relating to the shop is calculated at £250.

2   Rachel took fish from her shop throughout the year to eat at home. The purchases figure in the accounts of £30,000 is after deducting the £1,000 cost price of this fish. Rachel's normal mark-up is 100% on cost.

3   Capital allowances have been calculated at £2,500 for the accounting period.

required

Calculate the trading income assessment for Rachel.

solution

	£
Net Profit per accounts	5,738

Add Back:

Expenditure that is shown in the accounts but is not allowable

	£
Depreciation	1,250
Increase in General Bad Debt Provision	550
Capital expenditure (freezer)	1,000
Drawings	15,100
Personal pension contributions	400
Adjustment to reflect profit in goods taken for own use	1,000
	25,038

Deduct:

	£	
Income that is not taxable as trading income		
Building Society Interest Received	600	
Allowable expenditure not shown in accounts		
Electricity for business	250	
Capital Allowances	2,500	
		(3,350)
Trading Income Assessment		21,688

Note:

The adjustment for notional profit on the fish taken out of inventory is based on the normal mark up of 100% of cost. This increases the value of the fish taken out of the business to its normal selling price. The mark up could also have been calculated from the accounts, where gross profit/cost of sales = 100%.

If the transaction deducting the fish at cost from the purchases had not been recorded in the accounts already, a total adjustment of £2,000 would have been required.

CAPITAL ALLOWANCES UNDER INCOME TAX

You will be relieved to learn that the calculation of capital allowances for plant and machinery under Income Tax is nearly identical to the system under Corporation Tax. Before you study this section, you may find it useful to revise capital allowances as they apply to Corporation Tax.

These are the main issues that are important regarding the capital allowances for a sole trader or partnership.

- Capital allowances are calculated for the accounting period, and are treated as allowable expenditure. If the accounting period is for less than 12 months, or between 12 months and 18 months, writing down allowances only are time-apportioned. This is consistent with the treatment under Corporation Tax, although you will recall that CAPs over 12 months long do not exist under that system.

- The full expensing 100% first year allowance is only available for limited companies, and it cannot be claimed by sole traders or partnerships.

- The same annual investment allowance (AIA) that is available to limited companies is also available to sole traders and partnerships for acquisitions of plant and machinery. The limit of £1,000,000 for a 12-month period (time-apportioned for shorter or longer accounting periods) is also the same as for companies.

- Assets that have some private use by the owner(s) of the business (not employees) are treated in a special way for plant and machinery capital allowances purposes, since only the business proportion of any allowance can be claimed. The general rule is that any asset with part private use must be held in a 'single asset pool', and the initial calculations of the allowances and balances carried forward are carried out as normal. However, only the business proportion of all allowances and charges that apply to that asset can be claimed. So, a car with part private use would need to enter its own single asset pool. The writing down allowance on the car would be calculated as normal, but only the business proportion of the allowance would be claimed as a capital allowance.

Where a car or other asset with private use that is held in a single asset pool is disposed of, the pool must be closed. This will involve using a balancing charge or balancing allowance to bring the single asset pool balance to zero. Only the business proportion of the balancing charge or allowance will be accounted for in the capital allowances.

If an asset with part private use (other than a car) was acquired, then it would be entitled to the Annual Investment Allowance (AIA). However, only the business proportion of the AIA could be claimed. For the purpose of determining whether expenditure breaches the AIA limit, the whole of the expenditure on assets with part private use is counted – not just the business proportion. However, the taxpayer can choose which assets to claim AIA on if the total expenditure is over the limit.

This is an important practical difference between preparing capital allowances under Income Tax and Corporation Tax, and can cause confusion. Remember that companies do not have private use, and therefore no private use adjustment applies.

The 'small pools allowance' that can sometimes be used to write off the main pool or the special rate pool applies under Income Tax as well as Corporation Tax.

The structures and buildings allowance that is based on 3% per year of eligible expenditure works in exactly the same way for sole traders and partnerships as for limited companies.

We will now use a Case Study to illustrate some of the issues that we have discussed. When you are reading it, make sure, in particular, that you can understand how the private use of assets by the partners (or sole traders) affects the computation.

Case Study

CAPITOL IDEAS: CAPITAL ALLOWANCES

Capitol Ideas is the trading name of a partnership owned and run by James and Jo Capitol. The business produces accounts to 31 March each year. The adjusted trading profit for the accounting period of 12 months to 31/3/2024 has already been calculated at £84,000 before deduction of capital allowances for plant and machinery.

The capital allowance computation for the last accounting period closed with written down values as follows:

- main pool   £30,000

- single asset pool for car (a BMW) with 25% private use by Jo   £15,000

During the accounting period the following assets were acquired and disposed of:

- a new pick-up truck was bought for £20,000. This was to have 20% private use by James

- the BMW was sold for £14,000

- a used Audi car was bought for £25,000. This was to replace the BMW, and also had 25% private use by Jo. Emissions level is 45g/km

- a machine in the main pool was sold for £2,000

- a computer system was bought for £5,000

- a Ford car for staff use was bought for £11,000. Emissions level is 40 g/km

All disposal proceeds were less than original cost.

required

- Using a plant and machinery capital allowance computation, calculate the allowances for the accounting period y/e 31/3/2024.

- Calculate the adjusted trading profits for the accounting period (after capital allowances), and state for which tax year these will form the trading income assessable profits.

solution

The capital allowance computation is shown below. The notes that follow provide explanations.

	Main pool	Car (BMW) 25% private	Car (Audi) 25% private	Capital allowances
	£	£	£	£
WDV bf	30,000	15,000		
add				
Acquisitions				
without FYA or AIA:				
Ford Car (40 g/km)	11,000			
Audi Car (45 g/km)				
(25% private use)			25,000	
Acquisitions qualifying for AIA:				
Computer 5,000				
AIA claimed (5,000)	0			5,000
Pick up truck 20,000				
AIA claimed (20,000) × 80%				16,000
less				
Proceeds of Disposals:				
Machine	(2,000)			
BMW		(14,000)		
	39,000	1,000	25,000	
WDA 18%	(7,020)		(4,500) × 75%	10,395
Balancing Allowance		(1,000) ×75%		750
WDV cf	31,980	0	20,500	
Total Capital Allowances				32,145

- The only additions that do not attract AIA or FYAs are the two cars. The Audi has 25% private use so is kept separate, while the Ford joins the main pool. Both cars have emission levels of 50 g/km or less and so are entitled to 18% writing down allowances.

- The limit of AIA on purchases is £1,000,000. The £5,000 cost of the computer can be claimed in full, and the whole £20,000 cost of the truck is eligible for AIA. The £20,000 is then restricted for the 20% private use.

- The disposal proceeds of the machine are deducted from the main pool.

- The WDA on the Audi is £4,500 × 75% business use. Note that the full £4,500 is used to calculate the WDV carried forward.

- The disposal of the BMW was for less than the WDV brought forward. There is therefore a balancing allowance, but this is restricted to the business use of 75%. If a balancing charge had arisen, it would also have been restricted to the proportion of business use.

Calculation of trading income assessment:

	£
Adjusted trading profits (before capital allowances)	84,000
Capital allowances (as above)	(32,145)
Trading income assessment for tax year 2023/24	51,855

This amount will be then divided between the partners.

capital allowances when a business ceases

Capital allowances are calculated separately for each accounting period of a business, and the result forms part of the adjusted trading profits of each accounting period.

When a business ceases, plant and machinery capital allowances will need to be calculated for the final accounting period, but special care must be taken since:

- there can be no WDA, FYA or AIA in this last period

- all remaining assets will have been disposed of by the business

- balancing allowances and/or balancing charges will occur for all pools (including the main pool) since there can be no written down values to carry forward

Where there is partial private use of assets, any allowances or charges will need to reflect only the business proportion of the asset use. However, you may remember that balancing allowances and charges are not time-apportioned if we have long or short accounting periods, so at least that will not create a complication.

Any asset bought from the business by the owner of the business must be included as a disposal at open market value.

Case Study

S. TOPP TRADING:
CAPITAL ALLOWANCES AT END OF TRADE

Steve Topp has been running his business for many years, with an accounting date of 31 March.

The written down values carried forward at 31 March 2023 were:

Main Pool	£32,000
Car (80% business use)	£16,000

The business ceased trading on 30/6/2023.

Steve managed to sell all the remaining business assets (except the car) for £14,000. He bought the car from the business himself to use privately for a market value figure of £17,000.

r e q u i r e d

• Calculate the plant and machinery capital allowances for the accounting period 1/4/2023 to 30/6/2023.

s o l u t i o n

Plant & machinery capital allowances computation

	Main pool	Single asset pool car (20% private use)	Capital allowances
	£	£	£
WDV bf	32,000	16,000	
Disposals	(14,000)	(17,000)	
	18,000	(1,000)	
Balancing allowances	(18,000)		18,000
Balancing charge		1,000 × 80%	(800)
WDV cf	0	0	
Total Capital Allowances			17,200

structures and buildings allowance when business ceases

Structures and buildings allowance (SBA) is available for sole traders and partnerships as well as limited companies.

If a business has been claiming structures and buildings allowance, and the business ceases, the building will no longer be used by the business for a qualifying purpose. This means that the allowance will stop on the date that the business ceases (or earlier if the building is sold). The SBA may need to be time-apportioned if the last accounting period is less than 12 months.

Chapter Summary	
	▪ Trading profits of sole traders and partners are subject to Income Tax, and are included in their computations along with personal income. Evidence indicators called 'badges of trade' are used to establish whether an individual is trading or not.
	▪ The normal basis of assessment for the trading income of a business is the adjusted profits (after capital allowances) of the tax year. The accounts of sole traders and partnerships are tax-adjusted in a similar way to those of a limited company. Specific expenditure that is non-allowable in arriving at trading profit includes owners' drawings, private expenditure, and trading goods taken from the business for private use.
	▪ Capital allowances for plant and machinery can be claimed by the self-employed in a similar way to companies. Cars that have a private use element by the business owners need to be kept in a single asset pool, and only the business proportion of the capital allowances can be claimed. The business use part of other assets bought can form a claim for AIA or FYA. Full expensing allowances are not claimable by unincorporated businesses. Structures and buildings allowance is claimable in the same way as for limited companies.

Key Terms

badges of trade	indicators that are used to determine whether an activity constitutes trading, and should therefore be taxed as such
adjusted trading profits	trading profits that have been adjusted for tax purposes by excluding income not taxable as trading income and non-allowable expenditure
trading income assessment	the taxable trading profit for the tax year. It is made up of adjusted trading profits, after deducting any capital allowances
plant and machinery	one of the major non-current asset categories for capital allowance purposes. It includes vehicles and computers
annual investment allowance (AIA)	this is an allowance that can be claimed against the whole cost of most plant and machinery, with the exception of cars. The maximum that can be claimed is £1,000,000 for a 12-month period. This limit is reduced for shorter periods
first year allowances	100% First Year Allowances are available on new zero-emission cars in the CAP in which the acquisition takes place
writing down allowances	allowances are available at 18% of the pool value for plant and machinery. This figure relates to 12-month accounting periods, and is time-apportioned for shorter periods and longer periods up to 18 months. 6% writing down allowances are available on the balance on the 'special rate pool'
written down value (plant and machinery)	this term relates to the balance at the end of an accounting period that remains in a plant and machinery pool. It represents the part of the pool value that has not yet been claimed as allowances, and is carried forward to the next accounting period
balancing allowance (plant and machinery)	this allowance can be claimed when an asset is sold for less than the written down value (unrelieved expenditure) in a single asset pool
balancing charge (plant and machinery)	this is the opposite of an allowance, and occurs when the disposal proceeds of an asset in a single asset pool are more than the written down value (unrelieved expenditure). It is in effect a reclaiming of allowances previously obtained

Activities

6.1 Michelle Flatley has moved home seven times in the last five years, and currently lives in a house valued at £500,000. Her first property was a small studio apartment that she was left by her uncle. It was valued at £40,000. After carrying out some renovations she moved in, and stayed three months before selling the property for £60,000 and investing the proceeds in her next flat. She has continued this procedure with all the properties that she has owned, always renovating with a view to finding a prospective buyer, and always making a profit by timing the sale carefully. Michelle finances the purchases and renovations with short-term bank loans.

Required:

Using each of the 'badges of trade', explain the issues that provide evidence that she is trading, and those that point to non-trading.

6.2 The following items appear in a sole trader's income statement (profit and loss account), before the net profit figure. You are calculating an adjusted trading profit for tax purposes. State in each case whether:

- the item should be added to the net profit, or
- the item should be deducted from the net profit, or
- the item should be ignored

1 depreciation of vehicles

2 loss on sale of non-current assets

3 building society interest received

4 dividends received

5 owner's drawings

6 profit on sale of non-current asset

7 increase in general provision for bad debts

8 gifts of food hampers (with company adverts) to customers, costing £45 per recipient

9 decrease in specific bad debt provision

10 owner's self-employed National Insurance contribution

11 employers' National Insurance contributions regarding employees

12 owner's private expenses

6.3   Vikram Singh is in business as a sole trader. The unadjusted income statement for the year ended 31/3/2024 is as follows:

	£	£
Sales		700,000
less cost of sales		420,000
Gross profit		280,000
Bank interest received		12,000
Rental income		10,000
less expenses:		302,000
Salaries and wages	78,000	
Depreciation	22,000	
Loss on sale of non-current assets	4,000	
Administration expenses	11,600	
Advertising	8,000	
Overdraft interest payable	2,000	
Travel and entertaining	10,000	
Pension contributions	7,400	
Bad debts and provisions	15,000	
		158,000
Net Profit		144,000

Notes:
- Salaries and wages include £18,000 drawn by Vikram.
- Advertising includes:
  – gift vouchers given to 100 top customers £3,000
  – gifts of diaries with company logos to 200 other customers £1,000
- Travel and entertaining is made up as follows:

	£
Employees' travel expenses	2,000
Vikram's business travel expenses	3,500
Entertaining customers	4,500
	10,000

- Pension contributions consist of:

Contribution regarding employees	5,000
Contribution regarding Vikram	2,400
	7,400

- Bad debts and provisions is made up of:

Trade bad debts written off	10,400
Increase in specific bad debt provision	4,600
	15,000

- Capital allowances for the accounting period have been calculated at £23,000.

Required:

Adjust the net profit shown to arrive at the trading income assessment for the tax year 2023/24.

6.4 Candies & Cakes is the trading name of a shop owned and run by John Candy. The business produces accounts to 31 March each year. The adjusted trading profit for the accounting period of twelve months to 31/3/2024 has already been calculated at £12,000 before deduction of capital allowances for plant and machinery.

The capital allowance computation for the last accounting period closed with written down values as follows:

- main pool £25,000

- single asset pool for car with 40% private use by John £10,000

During the accounting period the following assets were acquired and disposed of:

- a new 'zero-emission' car was bought for £26,000. This was to have 40% private use by John

- the original car used partly privately by John was sold for £4,000

- a computer system was bought for £2,000

- a food processor was sold for £200

- a new shop counter was bought for £3,000

All disposal proceeds were less than original cost.

Required:

- Using a plant and machinery capital allowance computation, calculate the allowances for the accounting period y/e 31/3/2024.

- Calculate the adjusted trading profit or loss for the accounting period (after capital allowances).

6.5 Stan and Anne have run their partnership manufacturing business for many years, producing accounts up to the 31 March each year. At the start of April 2023 the following written down balances were brought forward for plant and machinery capital allowance purposes:

Main Pool	£66,300
Car (80% business use BMW)	£16,000

The income statement for the year ended 31/3/2024 was as follows:

	£	£
Sales		1,200,000
less cost of sales:		
Raw materials	300,000	
Direct labour	450,000	
Factory overheads	200,000	
	————	
		950,000
		————
Gross profit		250,000
less:		
Administration salaries	50,000	
Selling & distribution expenses	15,000	
Depreciation etc	40,000	
General expenses	35,000	
	————	
		140,000
		————
Net profit		110,000
		————

Notes:

- The direct labour relates to 20 employees of the partnership, and includes £5,000 employers' National Insurance contributions.

- The administration salaries include £20,000 drawn by Stan, and £25,000 drawn by Anne. All private motor expenses are included in these drawings.

- The 'depreciation etc' figure is made up as follows:

	£
Depreciation on plant & cars	32,000
Loss on sale of BMW car sold for £12,000	3,000
Depreciation on Factory	6,000
Gain on sale of Vauxhall car, sold for £4,000	(1,000)

- A used Range Rover (80% business use) was bought for £28,000 to replace the BMW. It has emissions of 200 g/km.

- A Ford was bought to replace the Vauxhall. It had 100% business use and cost £19,000. It has emissions of 40 g/km.

- There were no other acquisitions or disposals of non-current assets.

- General expenses include the following items:

	£
Bad Debts written off	3,000
Reduction in General Bad Debt Provision from £12,000 to £8,000	(4,000)
Office Party for all 20 employees	1,500
Entertaining customers	2,000

Calculate:

- The plant and machinery capital allowances for the accounting period.

- Trading Income assessment for the partnership for 2023/24, after incorporating the above capital allowances.

6.6 Mr Chang is a sole trader. His business has the following income statement:

	£	£
Sales		1,210,210
less Cost of sales:		808,480
Gross profit		401,730
less:		
Wages and salaries	125,778	
Rent, rates and insurance	59,221	
Repairs to plant	8,215	
Advertising and entertaining	19,077	
Accountancy and legal costs	5,710	
Motor expenses	53,018	
Telephone and office costs	14,017	
Depreciation	28,019	
Other expenses	92,460	405,515
Loss		(3,785)

Notes:

- Wages and salaries include: | | £
  - Mr Chang | 30,000
  - Mr Chang's wife, who works in the marketing department | 18,000

- Advertising and entertaining includes: | | £
  - Gifts to customers:
    - Bottles of wine costing £15 each | 2,250
    - 40 diaries carrying the business's logo | 400
  - Staff Christmas party for 20 employees | 1,485

- Motor expenses include those relating to: | | £
  - Delivery vans | 10,403
  - Sales manager's car | 6,915
  - Mr Chang's car expenses
  - (the car is only used for private mileage) | 5,700

- Other expenses include: | | £
  - Cost of staff training | 3,550
  - Subscription to a golf club for Mr Chang | 220

- Capital allowances have already been calculated at £9,878

Required:

Complete the adjusted trading profits / (loss) computation.

7 Income Tax – further issues

this chapter covers...

Firstly we will look at offset of trading losses for sole traders and partnerships. Here again there are similarities, but also important differences between the Income Tax rules and those for Corporation Tax.

The chapter then looks specifically at partnerships, and the rules for dividing the profits of the partnership between the partners is explained and illustrated. These include the rules that apply when partners join or leave a partnership.

The final section is concerned with a summary of penalties for non-compliance that apply to all incorporated businesses.

DEALING WITH TRADING LOSSES

In Chapters 2 and 5 we saw how trading losses for a limited company can be offset to reduce the amount of Corporation Tax that is payable. We will now examine the equivalent rules that apply to sole traders and partnerships under Income Tax. You will need to take particular care with loss provisions, since the rules under Income Tax and Corporation Tax are not identical, and this can lead to confusion.

In this section we will examine losses that occur in continuing businesses that are using normal twelve month accounting periods. If, once profits for an accounting period have been tax-adjusted and any capital allowances deducted, the result is a minus figure, a 'trading loss' will have arisen. This will have two implications:

- the trading income assessment for the relevant tax year will be zero (not the negative profit figure). This is the tax year in which the accounting period ends – ie the basis period

- the amount of the negative profit figure will form the trading loss, and the individual can choose how to set it off

The choices available are as follows:

1   The trading loss can be carried forward to reduce profits from the same trade in the future. If this option is chosen, the loss must be used up as quickly as possible. If the following year's profit from the same trade is less than the loss, then that profit will be reduced to nil and the balance of the loss carried on forward. This will occur as many times as is necessary to offset the whole loss.

2   The trading loss can be used to reduce (or eliminate) the total taxable income in the tax year of the loss. This set off would be against taxable income from all sources for the relevant tax year.

3   Whether or not option (2) above is chosen, the loss can be carried back against the total taxable income from all sources in the tax year preceding the tax year of the loss. If the taxpayer has sufficient loss and wishes to set against both these tax years, he/she can choose which year to set off the loss first.

Note that one important difference between Income Tax loss set off and the rules under Corporation Tax is that under Income Tax, the order of options 2 and 3 are entirely the taxpayer's choice.

Since the set offs under all the options take place before the personal allowance (currently £12,570) is deducted, there is a danger that this tax-free amount will be wasted in some situations.

The following diagram illustrates the main options using as an example a sole trader making up accounts to the 31 March each year. A loss arises in the year ended 31/3/2024, which is used for the tax year 2023/24.

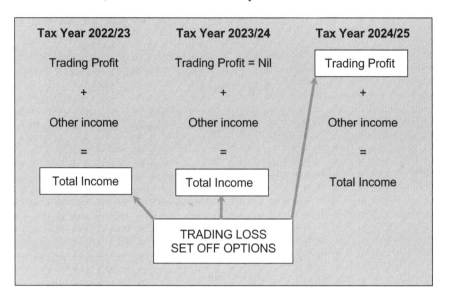

'Other Income' could include property income, employment income, savings income, and dividend income.

DOWNHILL TRADING:
TRADING LOSS OPTIONS

Downhill Trading is a business operated by Dawn Hill, who sells skiing equipment. The business has the following tax-adjusted trading results for the three twelve-month accounting periods to 31/3/2024. Dawn also has other taxable income for the tax years as stated below.

Accounting periods	y/e 31/3/22	y/e 31/3/23	y/e 31/3/24
	£	£	£
Trading Profit/(Loss)	12,000	(15,000)	16,000
Tax Years	**2021/22**	**2022/23**	**2023/24**
	£	£	£
Other Income	4,000	5,000	5,500

required

State the options available for offsetting the £15,000 trading loss incurred. Demonstrate the effects on the relevant total income figures, and comment briefly on the implications of each option.

solution

We will show the options one by one, but with all the three tax years' details shown in columnar form for reference. There are four options in this situation.

Option A

The trading loss could be carried forward and set against the trading income assessment of 2023/24. Since this profit is larger than the loss, the whole loss could be offset in this way. The three years would look as follows:

	2021/22	2022/23	2023/24
	£	£	£
Trading Profits	12,000	0	16,000
less loss relief			**(15,000)**
			1,000
Other Income	4,000	5,000	5,500
Total Income	16,000	5,000	6,500

An advantage of this option is that there is sufficient total income in each tax year to utilise at least some of Dawn's personal allowances. However, Dawn would have to wait until the tax for 2023/24 was payable until she felt the tax benefit of the loss in cash saved.

Option B

The trading loss could be set against the other income of the tax year of the loss (2022/23). Due to the size of the loss this will not be sufficient to offset the whole loss. The balance of the loss could then be carried back to the previous tax year and set against the total income. This would give the following figures.

	2021/22	2022/23	2023/24
	£	£	£
Trading Profits	12,000	0	16,000
Other Income	4,000	5,000	5,500
	16,000	5,000	21,500
less loss relief	**(10,000)**	**(5,000)**	
Total Income	6,000	–	21,500

A disadvantage of this approach would be that the personal allowance in 2022/23 is wasted, since there is no income in that tax year. However, Dawn would get a tax refund for 2021/22 almost immediately, assuming that she had already paid Income Tax based on total income of £16,000.

Option C

The trading loss could be set against the other income of the tax year of the loss (2022/23), as in option B. The balance of the loss could then be carried forward to the next tax year and set against the profits of the same trade only. This would give the following figures.

	2021/22	2022/23	2023/24
	£	£	£
Trading Profits	12,000	0	16,000
less loss relief			**(10,000)**
			6,000
Other Income	4,000	5,000	5,500
	16,000	5,000	11,500
less loss relief	–	**(5,000)**	
Total Income	16,000	–	11,500

A disadvantage of this approach would be that the personal allowance in 2022/23 is wasted, since there is no income in that tax year. Dawn would pay no tax for that year, but would have to wait to feel any further tax effect of the loss until payment of the 2023/24 tax.

Option D

The trading loss could be set against the other income of the previous tax year (2021/22). This would accommodate the whole loss. This would give the following figures:

	2021/22	2022/23	2023/24
	£	£	£
Trading Profits	12,000	0	16,000
Other Income	4,000	5,000	5,500
	16,000	5,000	21,500
less loss relief	**(15,000)**	–	
Total Income	1,000	5,000	21,500

A disadvantage of this approach would be that most of the personal allowance in 2021/22 is wasted, since there is only £1,000 of income in that tax year. However, Dawn would get a tax refund for the tax paid for that year almost immediately, assuming she had already paid Income Tax based on a total income of £16,000.

LOSSES IN OPENING YEARS OF NEW BUSINESS

In addition to the general options for offsetting losses that we have just examined, there is a special provision that is an option for trading losses incurred in any of the **first four** tax years of a new business.

When a loss is incurred in any of the first four years of the business, it can be offset against **total income of the three years before** the year of the loss. If this option is chosen, the loss must be first offset as far as possible against the **earliest** of these three years, and only then set against the next year, moving forward. This can be thought of as a FIFO basis.

When using this method of loss relief, there can be no safeguarding of the personal allowance, so just like the general carry-back provisions, the personal allowance may be wasted.

---

example

An individual started a new business in 2020/21. The adjusted trading income for the first years of trading were:

2020/21	Profit	£8,000
2021/22	Profit	£10,000
2022/23	Profit	£35,000
2023/24	Loss	(£40,000)
2024/25	Profit	£60,000

The individual had other income of £1,000 per year throughout this period.

If the carry back of losses option is chosen, then the impact on income would be as follows:

	2020/21	2021/22	2022/23	2023/24
	£	£	£	£
Trading Profits	8,000	10,000	35,000	0
Other Income	1,000	1,000	1,000	1,000
Loss relief	(9,000)	(11,000)	(20,000)	0
Total income	0	0	16,000	1,000

Direction of offset ⟹

Using this option would waste the personal allowance in both 2020/21 and 2021/22.

A better solution in this situation would probably be to use the general loss provisions outlined earlier, and to carry the loss forward against the trading profits of £60,000 in 2024/25. This would avoid wasting any personal allowance, although it would mean waiting longer for the cash benefit of the offsetting.

Where there are losses in more than one of the first four years of the business, and this option is chosen, then the claim for each year of loss is dealt with chronologically. This is logical, since the first loss to be incurred will be able to be carried back further than any subsequent losses.

This form of loss relief can be particularly useful if an individual has had a relatively high income from other sources before starting a new business, and it could save tax at a higher rate.

---

example

An individual started a new business in 2022/23, after leaving his job. He had earned £60,000 per year from employment (and was a higher rate taxpayer), but no other income in each of the previous three tax years.

The new business incurred trading losses of £15,000 in 2022/23 and £10,000 in 2023/24.

Using the carry back of losses, the loss of £15,000 could be fully offset against the total income of £60,000 in 2019/20. This would reduce his total income to £45,000 that year.

The loss of £10,000 incurred in 2023/24 could be carried back to 2020/21, and it would reduce that year's total income to £50,000.

Some of the tax saving would be at the higher rate.

LOSS ON CESSATION OF TRADE (TERMINAL LOSS)

Where a sole trader or partner ceases trading, and he/she incurs a trading loss in the final 12 months of the business, terminal loss relief can be claimed. This option is offered because the normal carry forward relief against profits of the same trade is impossible.

A trading loss incurred in the **final 12 months** can be relieved against trading income of the **three tax years before** the tax year of the loss, **latest year first**.

Notice that this differs significantly from loss relief for opening years. Terminal relief is offset against trading profits only (not total income). The order of offset under terminal relief is latest year first (i.e. LIFO), not FIFO.

---

example

A sole trader ceased trading in 2023/24. A terminal loss has been calculated relating to that tax year of £50,000.

The trading profits for the previous tax years were:

2020/21	Profit	£28,000
2021/22	Profit	£20,000
2022/23	Profit	£25,000

The individual also had other income of £15,000 each year.

Using terminal loss relief would provide the following results:

	2020/21	2021/22	2022/23	2023/24
	£	£	£	£
Trading Profits	28,000	20,000	25,000	0
Loss relief	(5,000)	(20,000)	(25,000)	
Other Income	15,000	15,000	15,000	15,000
Total income	38,000	15,000	15,000	15,000

Direction of offset ⇐══════════════

In this scenario, there is sufficient other income so that there is no wastage of the personal allowance. Using terminal loss relief, the loss can be offset in two earlier years than would have been possible under the normal loss provisions.

LOSS CLAIMS TIME LIMITS

The following is a summary of the key points under the various loss reliefs described in this chapter, together with details of when claims should be made.

Loss option	Claim limits
Carry forward against profits from same trade under general loss relief rules	Applies automatically to first available profits after other elections (if any)
Set against total income of current and/or previous year under general loss relief rules	Make claim by second 31 January following end of tax year of loss. 31 January 2026 for 2023/24 loss
Opening years loss option – set a loss in first four years of business against total income of previous three years, earliest year first	Make claim by second 31 January following end of tax year of loss. 31 January 2026 for 2023/24 loss
Terminal loss relief option – set a loss incurred in final 12 months of business against trading profits of previous three tax years, latest year first	Make claim within four years of the end of the tax year in which business ceases. 6 April 2028 for ceasing in 2023/24

DIVIDING TRADING PROFITS BETWEEN PARTNERS

We have seen throughout the last chapter that a partnership is taxed in the same way as a sole trader. It uses the same adjustment mechanism for trading profits, and capital allowances are calculated in exactly the same way.

The way in which partners decide to divide their profits is entirely their choice, and is stated in their partnership agreement. The division agreed will not only apply to the actual profits that the partnership generates, but also to the amount that is assessable on each partner for Income Tax purposes.

simple profit splits

If a partnership is made up of two individuals who agree to share profits and losses equally, then the calculation of each partner's trading income assessment is straightforward. The adjusted trading profits for the partnership (after capital allowances) is simply halved, and each partner is assessed on this figure.

So, for example, suppose the ongoing partnership of Sue and Adam had adjusted profits for the accounting period of 12 months to 31/3/2024 of £40,000 (after capital allowances). If their agreement was to divide profits and losses equally then the trading income assessment for Sue for the tax year 2023/24 would be £20,000, and the assessment for Adam for the same tax year would also be £20,000.

The simplest split is to agree a percentage that each partner will be entitled to. This could be a straightforward 50%:50% as just mentioned, or could be any other figures that the partners feel is fair. A partnership of three individuals may, for example, agree that a 60%:30%:10% split is fair in their particular circumstances. These divisions could also be expressed as ratios – 50%:50% would be shown as 1:1, while 60%:30%:10% could be expressed as 6:3:1.

more complex profit splits

Some partnerships may, however, agree a more complex division of profits and losses. They may for example agree that out of the profits:

- 'salaries' are to be provided for some or all partners, and/or

- 'interest on capital' should be paid to partners based on their investment in the partnership

Both these types of appropriation would be made out of the total profits that the partnership has made. The larger these payments are, the less profit will remain to be shared by the partners by using the agreed percentages or ratios.

For tax purposes the starting point would always be the adjusted profits of the accounting period (after capital allowances), and this is the amount that the combined trading income assessments of each partner must total. Any salaries or interest on capitals are allocated first, and then the remaining profit (or loss) is shared amongst the partners. Note that partners' salaries and interest on capitals are trading profits, and are taxed as part of trading income. Partners' salaries are not assessed as employment income, which only relates to employees.

If a profit sharing arrangement changes, the agreement that is in existence during the accounting period is the one that applies to dividing the tax-adjusted profits of that accounting period.

The Case Study that follows shows how individual partners' assessments are calculated for an ongoing partnership. We will then go on to look at some other situations.

Case Study

PENN, QUILL AND WRIGHT: PARTNERS' ASSESSMENTS

John Penn, Daisy Quill and Sue Wright have been trading in partnership for several years. The partnership produces accounts each year up to the 30 June. Their partnership agreement states that the following salaries, rates of interest on capitals, and shares of remaining profits or losses should apply:

	Salary (pa)	Interest on capital	Share of profit/loss
John Penn	£10,000	5%	30%
Daisy Quill	£15,000	5%	20%
Sue Wright	–	5%	50%

The partnership accounts for the twelve month accounting period to 30/6/2023 shows tax-adjusted profits of £95,000 (after deducting capital allowances):

The capital accounts balances for the partners are:

John Penn	£100,000
Daisy Quill	£50,000
Sue Wright	£250,000

required

Calculate the trading income for each of the three partners that will be based on the adjusted profits for this period.

solution

The following calculation shows how the adjusted profits are divided up:

	John Penn	Daisy Quill	Sue Wright	Total remaining
	£	£	£	£
Adjusted Profits				95,000
Salaries	10,000	15,000	0	(25,000)
				———
Balance Remaining				70,000
Interest on Capitals	5,000	2,500	12,500	(20,000)
				———
Balance Remaining				50,000
Share of Balance	15,000	10,000	25,000	(50,000)
	30,000	27,500	37,500	

The calculation follows the same principles that are used for dividing profits for financial accounting purposes (with which you may be familiar) – the only difference is that here our starting point is the adjusted profits after capital allowances.

Notes:

Salaries and interest on capitals are deducted from the original adjusted profit first, leaving a balance of £50,000 to be shared using the profit sharing percentages.

Interest on capitals are calculated using the individual partners' balances on their capital accounts.

The overall amounts allocated to each partner of £30,000, £27,500, and £37,500 total the original adjusted profit figure of £95,000.

The trading income for each partner will be:

John Penn	£30,000
Daisy Quill	£27,500
Sue Wright	£37,500

partnership losses

If a partnership incurs a trading loss, each partner's share of the loss can be dealt with independently. This means that each partner has the same choices of how their own share of the trading loss should be relieved as a sole trader. The individual partners could all choose different ways to relieve their own loss, according to their personal circumstances.

CHANGES IN A PARTNERSHIP

when the profit sharing agreement changes

Depending on when the existing partners decide to alter their profit sharing agreement, there are two possible implications:

- if the change is made with effect from a normal accounting date (ie the start/end of an accounting period), then the new arrangement will simply apply to the new accounting period.

- if the change is made during an accounting period, the adjusted profits (after capital allowances) will first have to be time-apportioned into the two parts of the period – before and after the change. Each part of the profits will then be divided amongst the partners according to the agreement in force at the time, and the two parts for each partner added together

when a new partner joins a partnership

When a new partner joins an established partnership (or a partnership is formed by an individual joining an established sole trader) the new partner is treated as if they had started a new business on the date that they joined. There will need to be a new profit sharing agreement that incorporates the additional partner, and this will operate from the date the new partner started.

If the new partner starts on a normal accounting date for the partnership, the situation is not too complicated, as the following example shows.

example: introduction of a new partner at the start of an accounting period

Rose and Daisy have been in partnership for several years, sharing profits and losses equally. They have always made their accounts up to 31 December each year. On 1 January 2023 they are joined by Bud, and the partnership agreement is changed to Rose 40%, Daisy 40%, Bud 20% from that date. They have never used salaries or interest on capitals as part of their profit sharing arrangement.

The first accounting year of the revised partnership (the year ended 31 December 2023) produced adjusted profits (after capital allowances) of £120,000.

For both Rose and Daisy their share of the profits for the y/e 31/12/2023 will be £120,000 × 40% = £48,000 each.

Bud will be treated as if he started a new business on 1 January 2023. His share of the profits for the accounting year ended 31/12/2023 will be 20% × £120,000 = £24,000.

a partner joining part way through an accounting period

If the new partner joins part way through an accounting period, the adjusted profits of the period must first be time-apportioned into the parts either side of that date. Each existing partner's assessment will then be generated by adding together their shares from each part of the period, just as if they had simply changed their profit sharing arrangement. The new partner will be treated as if he had started a new business on the date he joined. The following example will illustrate the situation.

example: introduction of a new partner part way into an accounting period

Oak and Ash have been in partnership for several years, sharing profits and losses equally. They have always made their accounts up to 31 December each year. On 1 October 2023 they are joined by Elm, and the partnership agreement is changed to Oak 40%, Ash 40%, Elm 20% from that date. They have never used salaries or interest on capitals as part of their profit sharing arrangement.

The year ended 31 December 2023 produced adjusted profits (after capital allowances) of £120,000.

The first step is to time-apportion the adjusted profits into the periods before and after Elm joined:

1/1/2023 – 30/9/2023	£120,000 × 9/12 = £90,000
1/10/2023 – 31/12/2023	£120,000 × 3/12 = £30,000

Oak and Ash

For the existing partners, Oak and Ash, they will each have a share of the profits for the whole accounting year made up of:

1/1/2023 – 30/9/2023	£90,000 × 50%	=	£45,000, plus
1/10/2023 – 31/12/2023	£30,000 × 40%	=	£12,000
			————
			£57,000

Elm

The new partner, Elm, will be treated as if he started a new business on 1 October 2023.

He has a share of the profits for the period 1/10/2023 – 31/12/2023 of

   20% × £30,000 = £6,000.

when a partner leaves a partnership

If a partner leaves then the treatment follows the same logic as we have just seen. The existing partners carry on as normal.

The following example illustrates the situation.

example: partner leaving a partnership

Reddy, Eddy and Go have been in business for several years, sharing profits equally, and making accounts up to 31 December. Go decides to leave the partnership on 30 June 2023.

The partnership had the following adjusted profits (after capital allowances) for their accounting periods:

1/1/2022 – 31/12/2022   £75,000

1/1/2023 – 31/12/2023   £60,000

After Go left the partnership, the remaining partners shared profits equally.

The division of profits for each accounting period will be as follows:

	Reddy £	Eddy £	Go £	Total £
y/e 31/12/2022	25,000	25,000	25,000	75,000
1/1/2023 – 30/6/2023	10,000	10,000	10,000	30,000
1/7/2023 – 31/12/2023	15,000	15,000		30,000
Total y/e 31/12/2023	25,000	25,000	10,000	60,000

change of partners with complex profit splits

We have now seen how complex profit splits can be dealt with, and how we manage changes in partners. If we need to deal with a situation that involves both these situations, the process is the same.

The following case study demonstrates how this is carried out.

Case Study

ALL CHANGE PARTNERSHIP COMPLEX CHANGES

Alison, Brian, and Carol have been in partnership for many years, with an accounting year end of 30 November. The adjusted profits of the partnership for the year ended 30 November 2023 was £240,000. On 30 June 2023 Carol decided to leave the partnership, and withdraw her capital. On the same date, Damon joined the partnership, and invested capital of £25,000.

The profit-sharing arrangements for the original partners were based on:

	Alison	Brian	Carol
Capital Invested	£50,000	£40,000	£50,000
Interest on capitals p.a.	8%	8%	8%
Salaries p.a.	£12,000	£6,000	£15,000
Share of profits	40%	30%	30%

At the date of the change of partners, Alison and Brian both increased their capitals by £10,000 each, and they continued with their previous salaries. It was also agreed that Damon would not receive a salary, and that all the partners would receive 8% interest on their capitals.

The new profit-sharing ratio for Alison, Brian and Damon was agreed as 45%, 35%, 20%.

required

Complete a table to show the allocation of each partner's profits. Round amounts to ensure that the totals agree if necessary.

solution

The procedure is to

• Time-apportion the year's profits into before and after the changes

• Calculate and allocate the salaries and interest on capitals

• Calculate the remaining profits for each period and allocate them.

	Alison	Brian	Carol	Damon	Total
	£	£	£	£	£
Period to 30 June					
Salary	7,000	3,500	8,750		19,250
Interest on capital	2,333	1,867	2,333		6,533
Profit Share	45,687	34,265	34,265		114,217
Total	55,020	39,632	45,348		140,000
Period to 30 November					
Salary	5,000	2,500		0	7,500
Interest on capital	2,000	1,667		833	4,500
Profit Share	39,600	30,800		17,600	88,000
Total	46,600	34,967		18,433	100,000
Total for year	101,620	74,599	45,348	18,433	240,000

INTEREST AND PENALTIES

Interest on tax is payable on late payments, and also on any underpayment of the amount due on account.

Penalties are also payable for:

1. Late submission of tax return:

- a £100 penalty for missing the deadline – regardless of the amount of tax involved

- for returns over three months late – an additional daily penalty of £10 per day up to a 90 day maximum of £900

- for returns over six months late – an additional £300 or 5% of the tax due if this is higher

- for returns over 12 months late – a further £300 or 5% of the tax due if this is higher if failure to file return is not deliberate

- for returns over 12 months late – a further £300 or 70% of the tax due if this is higher if failure to file return is deliberate but not concealed

- for returns over 12 months late – a further £300 or 100% of the tax due if this is higher if failure to file return is deliberate and concealed

There are very limited 'reasonable excuses' for late returns – for example, a fire or flood destroying paperwork or a serious illness.

The tax return submission deadlines are:

■ 31 October following end of tax year for paper-based returns

■ 31 January following end of tax year for online submission

2. Late payment of the balancing payment by more than 30 days:

■ 5% of the tax due plus

■ further 5% of the tax due if still unpaid by 31 July

■ a third 5% of the tax due if payment has still not been made 12 months after it was due

Note that the penalties are in addition to the interest charges.

incorrect returns

If after submitting a tax return, the taxpayer discovers that he has made an error or omission, he should notify HM Revenue & Customs as soon as possible. If the alteration results in less tax being payable than was originally thought, the taxpayer will receive a refund. Where additional tax is due this will of course need to be paid, plus interest that will run from the normal payment date.

If a taxpayer (or his agent) finds that they have made a mistake on a tax return, they have normally got 12 months from 31 January following the end of the tax year to correct it. For the tax year 2023/24 amendments can therefore be made by 31 January 2026.

HMRC can still be told about errors after the above date, but then the errors must be notified to HMRC in writing. Such notifications must be made within four years of the end of the tax year. This means the deadline relating to the tax year 2023/24 is 5 April 2028.

The following system for penalties applies for incorrect information stated in tax returns and documents. This is based on a percentage of the extra tax due, depending on the behaviour that gave rise to the error.

If the error is:

■ due to **lack of reasonable care**, the penalty is between 0% and 30% of the extra tax due

■ **deliberate**, the penalty is between 20% and 70% of the extra tax due

■ **deliberate and concealed**, the penalty is between 30% and 100% of the extra tax due

The penalty also depends on whether the disclosure was prompted or unprompted. This gives the following series of penalty rates:

Type of behaviour	Unprompted disclosure	Prompted disclosure
Reasonable care	No penalty	No penalty
Careless	0% to 30%	15% to 30%
Deliberate	20% to 70%	35% to 70%
Deliberate and concealed	30% to 100%	50% to 100%

The percentage can be reduced if the taxpayer tells HMRC about the error(s), helps HMRC work out the extra tax, and gives HMRC access to check the figures. If the taxpayer took 'reasonable care' there is no penalty.

These penalties also apply if a taxpayer fails to notify HMRC that he has self-employed income that is subject to tax.

This system also applies to Corporation Tax, as we saw earlier. The system for 'enquiries' is also the same as for Corporation Tax.

HMRC may open an enquiry into an individual or partnership tax return within 12 months of the submission of the return. If the enquiry leads to requests for documents from the taxpayer, and these are not submitted, there is an initial penalty of £300. This is increased by £60 per day that the failure continues.

failure to keep records

There can be a penalty for not keeping the required records for the correct length of time of up to £3,000 per tax year for individuals.

KEEPING RECORDS

Sole traders and partnerships need to keep records relating to their trading for five years after the online tax return is due to be submitted. For the tax year 2023/24 the return is due on 31 January 2025, and so the records must be kept until 31 January 2030. This date would be extended if HM Revenue & Customs were holding an enquiry into the taxpayer.

The records kept would be very similar to those retained by a limited company, as explained earlier. The records should be able to back up the information on the tax return, and would include:

- statement of profit or loss (income statement) and statements of financial position (balance sheets)

- cash books and bank statements

- account ledgers or working papers

- invoices relating to allowable expenses and the acquisition of non-current (fixed) assets

- non-current asset schedules

- taxation working papers, including capital allowance computations

- copies of tax returns

Chapter Summary

■ Where the adjusted trading profits (after capital allowances) result in a negative figure, the trading income assessment is zero, and a trading loss is formed that can be relieved in several ways. It may be carried forward and set off against the first available profits of the same trade. It may alternatively be set against the total income of the tax year in which the loss was incurred, and/or the previous tax year.

■ There are additional loss relief options for trading losses in the opening years of a new business, and for losses incurred in the final 12 months of a business that ceases.

■ Trading profits and losses for a partnership are divided amongst the partners according to the profit sharing agreement that is in force during the accounting period. This could include the allocation of salaries and/or interest on capitals, as well as a share of remaining profits or losses. These amounts all form part of the individual partners' trading income assessment.

■ There are various penalties and interest for late filing or payment, or for non-compliance with rules.

Key Terms		
	trading loss	this occurs when the adjusted trading profits after deducting capital allowances produces a negative figure. The negative figure is the trading loss, whilst the trading income assessment is zero
	loss relief	the offsetting of the trading loss against profits or total income etc according to legislation. This may be against future profits from the same trade, or against total income of the current and/or previous tax year
	opening years loss relief	optional loss relief available for losses incurred in the first four years of a business
	terminal loss relief	optional loss relief available for a loss incurred in the final 12 months of a business
	adjusted trading profits	the trading profits that have been adjusted for tax purposes by excluding income not taxable as trading income, and non-allowable expenditure
	trading income assessment	the taxable trading profit for the tax year. It is made up – after deducting any capital allowances – of adjusted trading profits for the tax year

Activities

7.1 Louise gave up her job on 31/3/2021 and started her business as a sole trader on 1/4/2021. She incurred a trading loss of £30,000 in 2023/24. Her income in recent years is as follows:

	2020/21 £	**2021/22** £	**2022/23** £	**2023/24** £	**2024/25** £
Trading income	0	12,000	14,000	0	20,000
Employment income	65,000	0	0	0	0

Explain briefly the options that Louise has for offsetting her loss, and recommend which will provide the greatest tax saving.

7.2 John, who had been trading for many years, ceased trading in 2023/24. He had a loss of £25,000 related to 2023/24 that qualifies as a terminal loss.

His trading income and other income for recent years is as follows:

	2020/21 £	**2021/22** £	**2022/23** £	**2023/24** £
Trading income	35,000	20,000	14,000	0
Other income	12,000	12,000	12,000	12,000

Explain briefly the options that John has for offsetting his loss, and recommend which will provide the greatest tax saving.

7.3 Alice and Bob have been in partnership for several years, sharing profits and losses equally. They have always made their accounts up to 31 December each year. On 1 October 2022 Colin joined the partnership, and the partnership agreement was changed to Alice 45%, Bob 40%, Colin 15% from that date.

The year ended 31 December 2022 produced adjusted profits (after capital allowances) of £96,000. The year ended 31 December 2023 produced adjusted profits (after capital allowances) of £108,000.

Required:

Calculate separately the trading profit for each of the partners for each accounting period.

7.4 Mark, Norma and Olga had been trading in partnership for many years, sharing profits and losses equally. They had always used 31 March as their accounting date. On 31 March 2024 Olga left the partnership.

The partnership accounts for the year ended 31/3/2024 were as follows:

	£	£
Sales		180,000
less cost of sales:		55,000
		————
Gross profit *less* expenses:		125,000
Rent	12,500	
Employees' Wages & NIC	16,500	
Depreciation	12,250	
Motor Expenses	8,000	
General Expenses	3,000	
Bank Interest	1,750	
	————	
		54,000
		————
Net Profit		71,000
		————

Notes:

1   There were the following written down values for plant and machinery capital allowances purposes as at 31/3/2023:

Main Pool   £35,000

Car (30% private use by Olga)   £16,000

Olga bought the car from the partnership on 31/3/2024 for the market value of £10,000. There were no other transactions in non-current assets during the period.

2   The motor expenses shown in the accounts include £500 relating to private mileage by Olga.

3   General Expenses include:

Increase in General Provision for Bad Debts   £200

Gift Vouchers as presents for customers   £400

Required:

•   Calculate the capital allowances claimable by the partnership for the accounting year ended 31/3/2024 (plant and machinery).

•   Calculate the adjusted profits for the same period, after taking into account the capital allowances.

•   Calculate the trading income assessment for Olga for 2023/24.

•   Calculate the Class 4 National Insurance contributions payable by Olga for 2023/24.

7.5 Shaun Slapp has been in business for many years as a self-employed plasterer, running his business from home. He produces accounts each year to 30 November. His accounts for the year ended 30/11/2023 are as follows:

	£	£
Sales		55,000
less cost of materials		11,000
Gross profit		44,000
less expenses:		
Van running costs	6,300	
Depreciation	2,800	
Wages of part-time employee	9,800	
Insurance	1,200	
Accountancy costs	600	
Entertaining	1,000	
Telephone and Postage	800	
		22,500
Net Profit		21,500

The van is used 20% privately, and the van expenses include this element. The telephone and postage costs are 75% business and 25% private. Capital allowances have already been calculated at £4,200 after taking account of private use of the van. It has been agreed that the amount of costs not shown in the above accounts that relate to heating and lighting the room in his house that is used as his business office is £150 per year.

Required:

Calculate the adjusted trading profits for the year ended 30/11/2023.

7.6 State whether each of the following statements is true or false in relation to general loss relief rules.

		True	False
(a)	A loss made by a sole trader can only be relieved against trading profits made in the same tax year.		
(b)	For a loss made by a sole trader to be relieved in the preceding tax year, it must first have been relieved in the current tax year.		
(c)	To be relieved in future years, a loss made by a sole trader must be relieved against the profits arising from the same trade.		
(d)	A loss made by a sole trader can be relieved against total income arising in future years.		
(e)	A sole trader can restrict the amount of loss carried back to any year so the personal allowances are not lost.		

7.7 Monica, Norman and Olga have been in partnership for many years, with an accounting year end of 31 August. The adjusted profits of the partnership for the year ended 31 August 2023 was £600,000. On 31 May 2023 Norman decided to leave the partnership, and withdraw his capital. On the same date, Paula joined the partnership, and invested capital of £60,000.

The profit-sharing arrangements for the original partners were based on:

	Monica	**Norman**	**Olga**
Capital Invested	£150,000	£80,000	£180,000
Interest on capitals p.a.	12%	12%	12%
Salaries p.a.	£36,000	£36,000	£48,000
Share of profits	40%	20%	40%

At the date of the change of partners, the continuing partners continued with their previous salaries. It was also agreed that Paula would receive a salary of £24,000 pa, and that all the partners would receive 12% interest on their capitals.

The new profit-sharing ratio for Monica, Olga and Paula was agreed as 30%, 40%, 30%.

required

Complete the table below to show the allocation of each partners' profits. Round amounts to ensure that the totals agree if necessary.

	Monica £	Norman £	Olga £	Paula £	Total £
Period to 31 May					
Salary					
Interest on capital					
Profit Share					
Total					
Period to 31 August					
Salary					
Interest on capital					
Profit Share					
Total					
Total for year					

8 Business disposals and tax planning

this chapter covers...

We will start this final chapter by examining how Capital Gains Tax impacts on the disposal of a business by an individual. This can apply to both unincorporated businesses, and to the shares in a personal limited company.

We will see how Business Asset Disposal Relief or Gift Relief can apply to these business disposals.

We will then go on to see how tax planning can be used to ethically minimise tax when structuring a business and when extracting profits. To do this we will see the impact of different taxes on businesses and their owners.

INTRODUCTION TO CAPITAL GAINS TAX

In the first section of this chapter we are going to see how the disposal of a business is subject to Capital Gains Tax. To do this, we will first explain the basics of the tax, and then go on to see how it applies specifically to the disposal of an unincorporated business, and to the disposal of shares held in a personal limited company.

basis of assessment

Capital Gains Tax is applied to individuals by using the same tax years as those used for Income Tax. The basis of assessment for Capital Gains Tax is the chargeable gains less capital losses arising from **disposals** that occur during the **tax year** (not in the basis period of the business). Both the definition of a disposal, and the types of asset that are exempt or chargeable are identical to those applicable under Corporation Tax. Most of the situations that we will come across will be based on the sale or gift of an asset. The interaction of capital allowances with chargeable gains is the same as was described for limited companies.

Two situations where disposals do not give rise to Capital Gains Tax are:

■ disposals arising because the owner has died

■ any disposal between spouses (husband and wife) or civil partners

HOW IS CAPITAL GAINS TAX CALCULATED?

annual exempt amount

Unlike limited companies, all individuals are entitled to an **annual exempt amount** (AEA) (or annual exemption) for each tax year. This works in a similar way to a personal allowance under Income Tax. The exempt amount is deducted from the total net gains that have been calculated on the individual assets that have been disposed of during the year. Capital Gains Tax is then worked out on the balance.

The exempt amount is £6,000 in 2023/24. The exempt amount can only be used against capital gains, and is not set against income. It cannot be carried back or forward and used in another tax year.

Once the exempt amount has been deducted from the total net gains, the balance is subject to Capital Gains Tax. The rates of Capital Gains Tax are 10% and 20% for gains on all assets with the exception of those relating to disposals of residential property (which we are not concerned with).

Although Capital Gains Tax is a separate tax from Income Tax, it uses the same band structure. Gains are treated as if they were added on top of taxable income. The 10% rate is applied to gains falling within the basic rate band and the 20% rate applies to gains within the higher or additional rate bands.

If an individual is already a higher rate or additional rate taxpayer then any gains will normally be taxed at 20%. Where the taxpayer pays Income Tax only at the basic rate then any gains will be taxed at the lower rates, provided they do not exceed the basic rate band of £37,700 when added to taxable income. Where they do exceed this amount the excess will be taxed at the higher rates.

The following example will illustrate the situation.

example

Raymond has total taxable income in 2023/24 of £33,200 after deducting his personal allowance. He made capital gains of £19,000 before deducting his exempt amount.

Raymond has taxable gains of £19,000 – £6,000 (exempt amount) = £13,000.

He has £37,700 – £33,200 = £4,500 remaining in his basic rate band after accounting for his taxable income. Therefore £4,500 of his gains will be taxed at 10%, and the remainder taxed at 20%, as follows:

£4,500 × 10%	£450.00
£8,500 (the remainder of the £13,000) × 20%	£1,700.00
Total Capital Gains Tax	£2,150.00

THE COMPUTATION OF EACH GAIN

The standard format that we saw in Chapter 4 in the treatment of Corporation Tax is largely applicable to disposals by individuals chargeable to Capital Gains Tax.

However, Capital Gains Tax computations for individuals are much simpler than the equivalent computations for companies, since for individuals there is no indexation allowance whatsoever.

The basic computation format is as follows:

		£
	Proceeds on disposal	X
	less	
	Incidental costs of disposal	(x)
=	Net proceeds	X
	less	
	Original cost	(x)
	Incidental costs of acquisition	(x)
=	Gain	X

transfer to spouse or civil partner

When an asset is transferred to a spouse or civil partner no capital gain arises, as mentioned earlier. This is achieved by treating the disposal proceeds as the amount needed to generate exactly zero gain or loss.

For example, if a wife bought an asset some time ago for £10,000 (with no other costs) and gave it to her husband, the disposal proceeds would be treated as £10,000 so that no gain would arise. This would also mean that if the husband later sold the asset, his cost would also be considered to be £10,000, and any gain calculated on that basis.

A transfer between spouses or civil partners is often known as being made on a 'no gain, no loss' basis.

chargeable and exempt business assets

The following assets are **chargeable** to Capital Gains Tax, and may be relevant to business disposals:

- Shares in a limited company
- Goodwill
- Land
- Buildings

If structures and buildings allowance (SBA) has been claimed on a building that is disposed of, the amount already claimed will be added to the disposal proceeds for Capital Gains Tax purposes. This will have the impact of increasing the gain.

Some plant and machinery can be chargeable to CGT. However, note that if an asset has had plant and machinery capital allowances claimed on it, then any loss on disposal will be dealt with through that computation, and a capital loss will not arise. It is unlikely that a gain would arise on plant and machinery.

The following relevant assets are **exempt** from Capital Gains Tax:

- Trading inventory
- Cars
- Cash
- Receivables

dealing with capital losses

Capital losses arise from disposals in the same way as gains.

Once losses have been calculated they are dealt with as follows:

- firstly they are set against gains arising in the same tax year, until these are reduced to zero, then

■ any unused loss is carried forward to set against the next gains that arise in future tax years

The key to offsetting losses is to remember that the order of calculation is:

1 firstly offset losses in the year

2 then deduct annual exempt amount

to arrive at the amount subject to Capital Gains Tax.

offsetting against gains arising in the same tax year

Any losses that arise during a tax year are offset against capital gains arising from disposals in the same tax year. When dealing with losses arising in the same tax year there can be no safeguarding of the annual exempt amount. If there are sufficient losses, the gains will be reduced to zero, wasting the exempt amount, before carrying forward any balance of loss.

offsetting against gains in a later tax year

This will only occur when there are insufficient gains in the same tax year to offset the loss (or no gains at all). The loss must be offset as soon as possible, by using any gains that occur in the next tax year. The system is very similar to the one just described, except that in these circumstances an amount of gain equal to the annual exempt amount is not offset, and any loss balance carried on forward again. This provides protection against wasting the exempt amount.

The Case Study that follows demonstrates the main issues that we have examined so far.

Case Study

JOHN GAIN TRADING: CAPITAL GAINS TAX

John Gain has been in business as a sole trader for several years. During the tax year 2023/24 he disposed of the following business assets:

He sold a piece of land for £20,000. He had bought the land in June 2000 for £30,000 and was originally going to extend his factory onto it. However, he was refused planning permission, and decided to sell it.

He sold a shop for £100,000. He had bought it for £72,000 in September 2005.

He sold a factory building for £300,000. He had bought it new in December 1990 for £120,000. John is a higher rate Income Tax payer. He has never claimed structures and buildings allowance.

required

Calculate the gain or loss on each disposal, and John's total Capital Gains Tax liability for 2023/24.

solution

Disposal of Land	£
Proceeds	20,000
less Cost	(30,000)
Loss	(10,000)

Disposal of Shop	£
Proceeds	100,000
less Cost	(72,000)
Gain	28,000

Disposal of Factory	£
Proceeds	300,000
less Cost	(120,000)
Gain	180,000

Summary	£
Gain on shop	28,000
Gain on factory	180,000
less loss on land	(10,000)
Net gains	198,000
less annual exempt amount (AEA)	(6,000)
Amount subject to CGT	192,000

Capital Gains Tax   £192,000 x 20% = £38,400

DEALING WITH THE DISPOSAL OF A BUSINESS

We have already seen how trading profits are calculated when a business ceases trading, and how the capital allowances for the last accounting period are calculated.

In addition to these implications, if a sole trader sells his or her business, then Capital Gains Tax will apply **individually** to **each chargeable asset** that is included in the business. The sale of the business can therefore result in a number of separate capital gains computations.

The current assets and current liabilities of a business are not chargeable assets, which leaves **non-current (fixed) assets** and **goodwill** as items on which CGT may be assessable.

non-current assets

As we have already seen, land and buildings are chargeable assets, and could easily form part of a business that is being disposed of. Cars are exempt. Other plant and machinery could theoretically give rise to a capital gain, but since it is rarely sold for more than it cost is unlikely to do so. Any plant and machinery disposed of for less than original cost would simply be dealt with through the capital allowances computation as we have seen previously.

goodwill

Goodwill is an intangible asset that may exist if the business is sold as a going concern. It arises when the buyer is prepared to pay more for the business as a whole than the market value of the net assets of the business. This could be, for example, because of the business's customer base that the new owner wishes to continue selling to. Where a sole trader has built up the business himself the goodwill is unlikely to be shown in the business statement of financial position (balance sheet), and will often have an original cost of zero for CGT purposes. If you are faced with a situation where the proceeds relating to the goodwill is not stated, you will need to calculate it as the balance of the proceeds that do not relate to any other assets.

BUSINESS ASSET DISPOSAL RELIEF

Business Asset Disposal Relief (previously known as Entrepreneurs' Relief) applies to individuals who dispose of:

- all or part of a trading business
- shares in a 'personal trading company'
- assets of an individual's or partnership's business that has now ceased

All assets must have been owned for at least 24 months prior to sale. The owner of shares in a personal trading company must have held the shares for at least 24 months and be employed in the company during that time.

The relief is available for qualifying gains up to a 'lifetime limit' and applies a tax rate of 10% to these gains (instead of 20%). The lifetime limit is £1,000,000 of gains.

Where qualifying gains occur (and are therefore taxed at 10% if within the lifetime limit) they are treated as using up the basic rate band. Therefore any other gains that do not qualify for Business Asset Disposal Relief will be more likely to be taxed at 20%. However, where there are both qualifying and non-qualifying gains, the taxpayer can set the annual exempt amount as far as possible against the non-qualifying gains. This will be most tax-efficient.

Claims for the relief must be made within 12 months of the online filing date for the tax year.

conditions for Business Asset Disposal Relief

The qualifying conditions have to have been met for at least a **two year** period that ends on the **earlier** of:

- the date of disposal of the asset(s)

- the date of cessation of the business

The conditions (which are summarised below) depend on the type of disposal:

- disposal of whole or part of a business

  The business must have been owned by the sole trader who is making the claim, or by a partnership of which the claimant was a member. The disposal must be of either the whole business or a distinct part of the business.

- disposal of assets following cessation of a business

  The business that has ceased must have been owned by the sole trader who is making the claim, or by a partnership of which the claimant was a member. The cessation of the business cannot be more than three years before the disposal of the assets.

- disposal of shares in a personal limited company

  The claimant must have held at least 5% of the ordinary shares in the company that provide entitlement to:

  - at least 5% of the voting rights, and
  - at least 5% of the company's distributable profits, and
  - at least 5% of the company assets available for distribution to equity holders in a winding up

The company must normally be a trading company, and the claimant must have been an officer or employee of the company.

<table>
<tr><td>**Case Study**</td><td></td></tr>
</table>

DUNN TRADING: DISPOSAL OF A BUSINESS

Jo Dunn had been in business as a sole trader since January 1995. She ceased trading on 31/1/2024, and on that date sold her business as a going concern for a total of £500,000.

The summarised statement of financial position of the business on 31/1/2024 was as follows:

	£
Premises	200,000
Plant & Machinery	20,000
Net Current Assets	80,000
Total Net Assets	300,000

The premises were bought in January 1995. No depreciation had been charged on the premises in the accounts. The plant and machinery value is based on amounts after depreciation had been charged. Capital allowances had been claimed on all plant and machinery.

It was agreed with the purchaser of the business that the premises were to be valued at £350,000 in the sale, and that the plant and machinery and the net current assets were valued at the amounts shown in the statement of financial position.

Jo has never made a claim for Business Asset Disposal Relief or Entrepreneurs' Relief before this disposal.

required

Calculate the CGT arising on the sale of the business, assuming that the disposals qualify for Business Asset Disposal Relief.

solution

The first step is to allocate the sale proceeds to the individual assets, including any balance of proceeds to goodwill, and determine which assets are chargeable.

	£	
Premises	350,000	Chargeable
Plant & Machinery	20,000	Proceeds < Cost. Dealt with through capital allowance computation
Net Current Assets	80,000	Exempt
Goodwill	50,000	Chargeable
Total Proceeds	500,000	

The goodwill is calculated as the balancing figure, after accounting for the other assets. The computations are then carried out individually on the chargeable assets.

Premises	£
Proceeds	350,000
less Cost	(200,000)
Gain	150,000
Goodwill	
Proceeds	50,000
less Cost	0
Gain	50,000
Summary	
Gain on premises	150,000
Gain on goodwill	50,000
Total Gains	200,000
less Annual Exempt Amount	(6,000)
Amount subject to CGT	194,000
CGT £194,000 × 10%	19,400

Since the total of qualifying gains is £200,000, this is below the lifetime limit of £1,000,000 and the gains are taxed at 10%.

DISPOSAL OF A PERSONAL COMPANY

We saw earlier that shares are a chargeable asset for Capital Gains Tax, and that the disposal of shares in a 'personal trading company' can qualify for Business Asset Disposal Relief.

example

John and Mary Powell are higher rate taxpayers. They started a limited company in 1995. As the only shareholders, they each invested £10,000 in ordinary £1 shares at par. They were both employed by the company, and ran it successfully until January 2024, when they decided to sell the company and retire. They accepted an offer of £12 per share for both shareholdings. They have never claimed Business Asset Disposal Relief previously, and have no other gains in 2023/24.

Since they are the only shareholders, they each own 50% of the company and have voting rights, entitlement to distributable profits, and entitlement to distribution of assets in a winding up. This gives them entitlement to claim Business Asset Disposal Relief.

The Capital Gains Tax for **each** individual will be calculated as:

	£
Disposal proceeds (10,000 shares at £12)	120,000
less Cost	(10,000)
Gain	110,000
less Annual Exempt Amount	(6,000)
Amount subject to CGT	104,000
CGT £104,000 x 10%	10,400

GIFT RELIEF

We saw earlier in our studies that the gift of an asset is a disposal for Capital Gains Tax purposes. This means that even though the donor (the person giving the item) has received nothing for the item, he/she may still have to pay CGT. The disposal will be treated as if the donor had received the market value for the item, and the recipient will be treated as if he/she had acquired the asset at the same market value.

If an individual gives away a 'business asset', the transaction can qualify for 'gift relief'. This has the effect of delaying the onset of the tax, and transferring the liability to the recipient of the gift.

The relief can only be claimed if both parties agree. It means that the donor has no CGT liability, but that the CGT liability of the recipient in the future could be greater – if the item is disposed of.

Gift relief works by reducing the base cost of the asset for the recipient by the amount of the deferred gain. This means that the base cost would now be the market value less the deferred gain, and any eventual gain would therefore be greater than if gift relief had not been claimed.

Gift relief applies to business assets, including:

- assets used in the donor's business or in his/her personal trading company
- shares in the donor's personal trading company
- unquoted shares in other trading companies

Gift relief applies to some of the same business assets as Business Asset Disposal Relief. It is therefore possible that where an asset incorporating a gain deferred by gift relief is disposed of again, the gain could be subject to Business Asset Disposal Relief.

Case Study

JAN NICE: GIFT RELIEF

Jan Nice bought a shop in October 1998 for £100,000, and used it in her business until June 2007, when she gave it to her niece, Norah. The market value of the shop at that time was £180,000.

Norah ran the shop as a sole trader for a while, but decided to sell the shop in October 2023. She received £220,000 for the shop.

Jan and Norah claimed gift relief on the shop. Norah had no other disposals in 2023/24.

Norah is a higher rate Income Tax payer.

required

Calculate the Capital Gains Tax payable by Norah on her disposal of the shop:

(a) ignoring any Business Asset Disposal Relief

(b) assuming that Norah is entitled to Business Asset Disposal Relief

solution

(a) The gain deferred by Jan is (£180,000 – £100,000) = £80,000.

The disposal by Norah will have the following gain:

		£	£
Proceeds			220,000
less	Market value at acquisition	180,000	
	less deferred gain	(80,000)	
			100,000
Gain			120,000
less annual exempt amount			(6,000)
Amount subject to CGT			114,000
Capital Gains Tax	£114,000 × 20% =		22,800

(b) If Business Asset Disposal Relief is available, the calculation would be identical up to the point where the amount subject to CGT is calculated. It will then be as follows:

Amount subject to CGT		£114,000
Capital Gains Tax	£114,000 × 10% =	£11,400

PROCEEDS RECEIVED AFTER DISPOSAL

Sometimes, proceeds can be received after the business disposal. The way that these are dealt with will depend on the circumstances.

■ Trading income from an unincorporated business

If additional trading income is received after an unincorporated business has ceased trading, then it will be taxed in the year that it is received, under Income Tax. This could occur, for example, if a written off bad debt was recovered. The taxpayer can make an election to treat the amount as received in the year that the business ceased, provided the receipt is within six years of the business ceasing.

■ Business disposal receipts paid in instalments

It may be agreed between the buyer and the seller that the proceeds will be paid in instalments. In this situation, the future instalments will be included in the total disposal proceeds, and they will be used in the calculation of the original capital gain.

■ Proceeds of shares partly dependent on future performance

It is possible that an agreement to sell a limited company could include a provision to make a further payment if the company achieves a certain performance level. In this situation, the expected additional proceeds will normally be included in the original gain calculation. A subsequent capital gain (or loss) could then occur later if the proceeds were not as expected.

PAYMENT OF CAPITAL GAINS TAX

Capital Gains Tax is payable as one amount on the 31 January following the end of the tax year. This is the same date as the final submission date of the online tax return (the paper-based tax return would be due by the preceding 31 October). There is no requirement for payments on account of CGT.

KEEPING RECORDS

Since capital gains can arise when assets that have been held for a considerable time are disposed of, this has implications for record keeping. Taxpayers need to plan ahead, and retain records relating to the acquisition of assets that will be chargeable if disposed of.

Typical records that should be kept include:

■ contracts, invoices or other purchase documentation relating to the acquisition of assets

■ details of any valuations (eg valuations relating to part disposals)

■ documentation relating to the sale of assets

Records for CGT purposes should be retained for the same period of time as those relating to Income Tax. For those in business this is five years after the date that the online return must be submitted (eg for 2023/24, records should be kept until 31/01/30). Where records will also relate to later disposals – for example, gift relief claims and Business Asset Disposal Relief claims – they will need to be retained until all the relevant assets have been disposed of.

TAX PLANNING FOR BUSINESSES

In this final section of the book we are going to examine some opportunities for ethical tax planning by business owners. The fundamental choice facing new business owners is the structure of the business. There are many implications, both relating to tax and relating to other issues, that can inform the decision as to whether a business is developed as an unincorporated business (e.g. a sole trader) or a limited company. In this section we are only considering small limited companies – family companies, or those with very few shareholders. We will start by discussing the tax rates that apply to profits earned in different business structures.

tax rates for different business structures

■ **Sole traders**

As we have seen, the profits from self-employment are taxed under Income Tax and form part of the personal income of the business owner. The following rates and bands apply to self-employed profits after the personal allowance of £12,570 has been deducted.

Basic rate	to £37,700	20%
Higher rate	£37,701 to £125,140	40%
Additional rate	over £125,140	45%

In addition to Income Tax, the profits of sole traders are subject to Class 2 and Class 4 National Insurance contributions at the following rates:

Class 2 contributions	£3.45 per week
Class 4 contributions	9% of trading profits from £12,570 to £50,270, plus 2% of trading profits over £50,270.

Since the personal allowance of £12,570, plus the basic rate band of £37,700 totals £50,270, we can see that, for profit levels above £12,570, the combined effect of Income Tax and Class 4 National Insurance is:

Profits to £50,270	20% + 9% = 29%
Profits £50,271 to £125,140	40% + 2% = 42%
Profits over £125,140	45% + 2% = 47%

These percentages may provide a useful comparison when considering different business structures.

It is also worth pointing out that the level of drawings (the amount taken out of the sole trader business by the owner) has no impact on the amount of Income Tax and National Insurance. The profits are subject to tax on the individual, regardless of whether all or none of the profits are taken out of the business.

Limited companies

As we learnt earlier, the Corporation Tax rates for Taxable Total Profits of limited companies are 19% if annual profits are up to £50,000, 25% if annual profits are over £250,000, and 25% less marginal relief if annual profits are between these two levels. This assumes there are no associated companies. Because of the way that marginal relief is calculated, the effective marginal rate of tax between £50,000 and £250,000 is 26.5%. This means that any additional profit in this band increases tax by 26.5%, while any profit reductions reduce tax by 26.5%.

A limited company has a separate legal existence to its owners, and the Corporation Tax is payable by the company itself. It is then a separate issue for the business owners to extract profits from the company.

There are two main ways that the owners of a limited company can extract profits, and each has different tax implications.

Salaries of owners

The company owners can choose to employ themselves in the company, and then arrange for the company to pay them salaries. This is provided that the individuals carry out work for the company that is commensurate with the salary level. Salaries must be carried out through Pay as you Earn (PAYE). Payment of salaries has important implications:

- The company will need to pay employers' National Insurance contributions at 13.8% on individual salaries above £9,100 pa

- The company can deduct both the salaries and the employers' NIC in the calculation of profits subject to Corporation Tax

- The individual will pay Income Tax on the salary at the same rates as described for sole traders

- The individual will also pay employees NIC at 12% of salary between £12,570 and £50,270, and 2% above £50,270

There is an employment allowance of up to £5,000 in total per year that a company can set against employers' NIC, unless the company only has one employee, who is also a Director.

■ **Dividends to shareholders**

The company owners can choose to pay dividends to shareholders. The tax implications of extracting profits through dividends are quite different from salaries:

- There are **no** National Insurance implications for the company or the individual shareholder

- The company **cannot** deduct the dividends paid in the calculation of profits subject to Corporation Tax

- The individual shareholder will pay Income Tax on the dividends after deducting the personal allowance (and a dividend allowance of up to £1,000) at the following rates:

to £37,700	8.75%
£37,701 to £125,140	33.75%
over £125,140	39.35%

Notice that these rates are lower than the equivalent rates for self-employment and employment.

comparing tax implications

As can be seen from the above data, it is not straightforward to compare the tax implications of different business structures and extraction of profits. You will not be asked to carry out Income Tax computations in your examination, but you may be asked to discuss the key aspects and make broad comparisons.

■ **Sole trader profits compared with limited company salary**

Since both these options involve Income Tax at the same rates but National Insurance contributions at different rates, a comparison can be carried out. It can be seen that the tax burden on the individual of Income Tax plus National Insurance is **greater for a limited company employee** due to employees NIC being 12% (up to £50,270) compared with 9%. In addition, there will also be employers NIC for the company to pay.

If salaries were utilised in a limited company to extract **all** the profits, there would be no Corporation Tax liability on the company, although this would be difficult to manage in practice. However, using a limited company structure will provide more flexibility, since some profits can be left in the company, reducing the Income Tax and NIC levels. While salaries attract Income Tax and NIC, retained profits attract Corporation Tax.

■ **Comparison with company dividends**

Since dividends are not tax-deductible in the Corporation Tax computation, we must be careful in our comparison with other mechanisms. Dividends will be paid out of company profits on which Corporation Tax will also be paid. In order to obtain a fair comparison, both the Income Tax and Corporation Tax burden would need to be calculated. These calculations are beyond the scope of your current studies. It is sufficient to point out at this stage, that the most tax-efficient option would depend on the individual personal circumstances and the amounts being considered.

cash flow implications of different taxes

We have noted above how different taxes impact on the business structures and methods of extraction of profits. It is worth bearing in mind when the various taxes need to be paid, as this can have an effect on the cash flow of the business and the individual.

■ **Income Tax and NIC for self employed**

You will recall that the final date for payment is 31 January following the end of the tax year. There may also be payments on account based on the previous year's data.

■ **Corporation Tax**

As we have seen earlier this is due nine months and a day after the end of the CAP.

■ **Income Tax and NIC on Salaries**

The Income Tax and NIC (both employees' and employers') is payable on a monthly basis throughout the period. The employee will receive a net figure under PAYE.

■ **Income Tax on Dividends**

Income Tax on dividends is paid under self-assessment. Final date for payment is 31 January following the end of the tax year.

Note in the above list the key difference for the individual between payment of tax when receiving a salary from a company, and when receiving dividends.

extracting profit for spouses / civil partners

The discussion above about methods of extracting profits also generally applies to spouses or civil partners who are involved in a business.

■ **Unincorporated business**

A sole trader could employ a spouse (or other family member) in the business, and then pay them a salary. The work must be in line with the pay level to be acceptable by HMRC. PAYE would need to be operated, and employers' NIC would apply. The salary and employers' NIC would be deductible in the calculation of tax-adjusted profits for the sole trader.

This may be particularly useful if the spouse is a basic rate taxpayer (or even a non-taxpayer), but the sole trader is a higher rate taxpayer, since it can reduce the total liability of the couple. It can also ensure that no personal allowance is wasted.

An alternative to employment would be to convert a sole trader business into a partnership with the spouse. The split of profits could be as they wished. In this case PAYE would not be operated, and both partners would pay Income Tax and Class 2 and 4 NIC in the same way as a sole trader. This would be more tax-efficient in most situations than using employment.

■ **Limited company**

The same mechanisms of salaries and/or dividends could be used for spouses or civil partners as would apply to other business owners. If paying a salary, then the pay should be commensurate with the level of work. Any dividends paid would have to be based on the shareholding of the spouse. Since gifts of shares between a married couple (or civil partners) are exempt from tax, this should be straightforward to organise.

The allocation of profit extraction between couples will again be most useful where they each pay Income Tax at different rates, and this can be taken advantage of, along with utilising both personal allowances.

Chapter Summary

- Capital Gains Tax applies to individuals (including sole traders and partners) who dispose of chargeable assets. In this unit we are concerned with the disposal of business assets.

- Where a whole business is disposed of, a separate computation is carried out for each chargeable asset that is included in the business. This includes goodwill, which is an intangible asset that may arise when the business is sold as a going concern. These gains may have Business Asset Disposal Relief available.

- Gift relief is available on the gift of business assets where both parties agree. It has the effect of deferring the gain, so that the donor is not subject to CGT, but the recipient may pay more tax if the asset is subsequently disposed of.

- CGT is payable on the 31 January following the tax year. Records must be kept for five years after that date, or longer if they relate to assets that are still owned or subject to deferral relief.

- Earning profits and extracting them in different business structures can involve Income Tax, Corporation Tax and National Insurance Contributions in various ways. Care should be taken to understand the tax implications and carry out tax planning.

Key Terms		
	Capital Gains Tax (CGT)	the tax that applies to individuals who dispose of chargeable personal or business assets
	disposal	a disposal for CGT purposes is the sale, gift, loss or destruction of an asset
	chargeable asset	assets whose disposal can result in a CGT liability. All assets are chargeable unless they are exempt
	exempt asset	an asset that is not chargeable to CGT. Exempt assets include the current assets of a business
	annual exempt amount (AEA) (or annual exemption)	the amount that is deductible from an individual's net gains in a tax year before CGT is payable
	capital loss	a capital loss results when the allowable costs of an asset exceed the sale proceeds (or market value). A loss is used by setting it against a gain in the same year, or if this is not possible, by carrying the loss forward to set against gains in the next available tax year
	goodwill	goodwill is a chargeable asset. It is the amount of the proceeds on disposal of a business that does not relate to any individual assets, but is instead due to the intangible value of the business as a going concern
	gift relief	a relief claimable jointly by the donor and the recipient of certain assets, including business assets. It allows the original gain by the donor to be deferred by increasing the possible future gain of the recipient
	Business Asset Disposal Relief	this relief applies to individuals who dispose of all or part of a trading business and/or shares in a 'personal trading company'. The relief works by charging CGT at 10%. It is subject to a lifetime limit of £1m gains

Activities

8.1 Analyse the following list of business assets into those that are chargeable to CGT and those that are exempt.

		Chargeable	Exempt
(a)	Cash		
(b)	Trading inventory (stock)		
(c)	Shares in CIC plc		
(d)	An office block		
(e)	Goodwill		
(f)	Land		
(g)	A car		
(h)	Receivables		

8.2 Vikram is a sole trader. In January 1995 he bought a small shop for £60,000. He sold the shop for £140,000 in July 2023. This was his only disposal in the tax year. Vikram is a higher rate Income Tax payer.

Required:

Calculate the amount of Capital Gains Tax payable by Vikram for 2023/24, assuming that:

(a) Business Asset Disposal Relief does not apply.

(b) Vikram is entitled to Business Asset Disposal Relief.

8.3 In January 1995 George bought an office building to use in his business. In December 2000 he gave the office building to his son, William, who used it in his business. The building was valued at £100,000 at that time, and they claimed gift relief on the transaction, deferring a gain of £33,160. William sold the building for £200,000 in July 2023. This was his only disposal in 2023/24. William is a higher rate Income Tax payer.

Required:

Calculate the amount of Capital Gains Tax payable by William for 2023/24, assuming that:

(a) Business Asset Disposal Relief does not apply.

(b) William is entitled to Business Asset Disposal Relief.

8.4 Josie started a business as a sole trader in January 1990. She ceased trading on 31/1/2024, and on that date sold her business as a going concern for a total of £1,900,000.

The summarised statement of financial position of the business on 31/1/2024 is as follows:

	£
Premises	340,000
Plant & Machinery	30,000
Net Current Assets	50,000
Total Net Assets	420,000

The premises were bought in January 1999. The amount shown represents the actual cost in 1999 of the current premises.

The plant and machinery is shown at cost minus depreciation to date. Capital allowances had been claimed on all plant and machinery.

It was agreed with the purchaser of the business that the premises were to be valued at £1,700,000 in the sale. The plant and machinery is valued at £20,000 in the sale, and the net current assets are valued at the amounts shown in the statement of financial position.

Required:

Calculate the Capital Gains Tax liability arising on the sale of the business, assuming that Business Asset Disposal Relief **is available**. Josie has not made any previous claims for Business Asset Disposal Relief. Josie is a higher rate tax payer.

8.5 Which of the following statements is correct?

(a)	A capital loss made by an individual can be carried back against capital gains made in the preceding tax year	
(b)	A capital loss made by an individual can be carried forward to the following tax year without offsetting it against the current year gains	
(c)	When a capital loss made by an individual is offset against gains in the following tax year, it is only to the extent that it reduces those gains to the amount of the annual exemption	
(d)	A capital loss made by an individual can only be carried forward for one tax year	

8.6 John made a disposal in August 2023 that qualified for Business Asset Disposal Relief. The proceeds were £600,000 and the gain was calculated as £300,000.

John is a higher rate Income Tax payer. This was John's only disposal in the tax year. He had claimed Business Asset Disposal Relief in the previous tax year on gains of £500,000.

How much Capital Gains Tax will John need to pay in 2023/24?

(a)	None	
(b)	£29,400	
(c)	£30,000	
(d)	£40,000	
(e)	£58,800	
(f)	£84,000	

8.7 **(a)** Analyse the following expenditures into those that are tax-deductible in the calculation of assessable trading income in an unincorporated business, and those that are not.

Expenditure	Tax-deductible	Not tax-deductible
Drawings of sole trader		
Agreed salary of sole trader's spouse		
Salaries of partners		
Salary of sole trader		

(b) Analyse the following expenditures into those that are tax-deductible in the calculation of assessable trading income in a limited company, and those that are not.

Expenditure	Tax-deductible	Not tax-deductible
Dividends		
Agreed salary of shareholder's spouse		
Salaries of directors		

8.8 David and Sue are a married couple. David runs his business as a sole trader, and Sue acts as (currently unpaid) administrator for the business. The profits for the business are approximately £65,000 per year. Neither David or Sue have income from any other source.

They are considering bringing Sue formally into the business, either as:

An employee earning £20,000 per year, which is considered in line with the work carried out, or

As a partner entitled to 30% of the business profits

Explain the impact in terms of Income Tax and National Insurance Contributions on both David and Sue of each option. You do not need to carry out calculations.

Answers to chapter activities

CHAPTER 1: INTRODUCTION TO BUSINESS TAXATION

1.1 The following statements are true: **(a), (d), (e).**

The other statements are false as follows: (b) the Finance Act is not the only relevant law. (c) the return is completed for each CAP, not each financial year. (f) It is unethical to bend rules or omit items. (g) The self-employed do not pay Income Tax under PAYE.

1.2 **(a)** **Corporation Tax Computation for DonCom plc for year ended 31/3/2024**

	£
Trading Profits	1,300,000
Income from Property	100,000
Chargeable Gains	500,000
Taxable Total Profits (TTP)	1,900,000
Corporation Tax on TTP (£1,900,000 × 25%)	475,000

Note: Taxable Total Profits is also known as PCTCT.

(b) | Filing date for CT600 return | 31/3/2025 |
|---|---|
| Final Payment date for Corporation Tax | 1/1/2025 |

1.3 **(a)** **Income Tax Computation for 2023/24**

	£
Trading Income (Share of Partnership Profits)	16,000
Other Taxable Income	2,000
	18,000
less personal allowance	12,570
Taxable Income	5,430
Tax payable at 20%	1,086

(b) A paper-based return must be submitted by 31/10/2024 whether or not HM Revenue & Customs is to calculate the tax.

Final payment date is 31/1/2025.

1.4 **John**

		£
Class 2	£3.45 × 52 weeks	179.40
Class 4	(£25,000 – £12,570) × 9%	1,118.70
		1,298.10

Class 2 and Class 4 is paid with the Income Tax liability.

1.5 The Walvern Water Company Limited will require a company tax return (form CT600). This will relate to the Chargeable Accounting Period (CAP) 1/8/2022 to 31/7/2023. The form must be submitted online by 12 months after the end of the accounting period, ie 31/7/2024. The final Corporation Tax payment must be made by 1/5/2024 (nine months and one day after the end of the CAP).

Wally Weaver will need a tax return for the tax year 2023/24. The accounting period of 1/4/2023 to 31/3/2024 will form the period for this tax year. The main part of the form will need to be completed. The online tax return must be submitted by 31/1/2025. The final Income Tax payment relating to 2023/24 will also need to be made by 31/1/2025.

1.6 **(1)** (d) An individual failing to keep appropriate records for the correct length of time is subject to a penalty of up to £3,000 for each tax year.

(2) £70,000 – £50,270 = £19,730

(3) (£35,000 – £12,570) × 9% = £2,018.70

1.7

Payment date	31 Jan 2023 £	31 July 2023 £	31 Jan 2024 £	31 July 2024 £	31 Jan 2025 £	31 July 2025 £
Tax year 2022/23	0	0	6,200	0	0	0
Tax year 2023/24	0	0	3,100	3,100	4,800	0
Tax year 2024/25	0	0	0	0	5,500	5,500
Totals due	0	0	9,300	3,100	10,300	5,500

CHAPTER 2: CORPORATION TAX – TRADING PROFITS

2.1 **1** no action (allowable)

2 add back (disallowable expense)

3 deduct (not trading income)

4 deduct (not taxable income)

5 no action (allowable)

6 deduct (not trading income – possible chargeable gain)

7 no action (taxable trading income)

8 add back (disallowable expense since tobacco)

9 add back (disallowable expense – not specific)

10 add back (disallowable expense – not trading)

11 no action (allowable)

12 add back (charge against whole TTP)

2.2

	£	£
Net Profit per accounts		130,300
Add Back:		
Expenditure that is shown in the accounts but is not allowable		
Depreciation		42,000
Loss on Sale of Non-current Assets		5,000
Gifts of Chocolates		4,900
Entertaining Customers		6,000
		188,200
Deduct:		
Income that is not taxable as Trading Income		
Interest Received	20,000	
Dividends Received	70,000	
Decrease in General Bad Debt Provision	5,000	
Capital Allowances	23,000	
		(118,000)
Trading Income Assessment		70,200

2.3

	£	£
Net Profit per accounts		276,600
Add Back:		
Expenditure that is shown in the accounts but is not allowable		
Depreciation		51,000
Directors' Speeding Fines		2,000
Gift Vouchers		5,000
Entertaining Customers		4,000
		338,600
Deduct:		
Income that is not taxable as Trading Income		
Interest Received	40,000	
Gains on Disposal of Non-current Assets	50,000	
Rental Income Received	60,000	
Capital Allowances	31,500	
		(181,500)
Trading Income Assessment		157,100

2.4

		£
Net Profit for 16-month period per accounts		4,070
Add back non-allowable expenditure:		
Depreciation etc		10,000
Entertaining customers		1,930
Adjusted profit before capital allowances		16,000
Time-apportionment of adjusted profit:		
CAP 1/12/2022 to 30/11/2023	£16,000 × 12/16	= £12,000
CAP 1/12/2023 to 31/3/2024	£16,000 × 4/16	= £4,000

Deduction of Capital Allowances:	1/12/22 – 30/11/23	1/12/23 – 31/3/24
	£	£
Adjusted profit	12,000	4,000
Capital allowances	(8,000)	(2,500)
Trading Income assessment	4,000	1,500

2.5

	£	£
Profit before Tax		294,000
Add Back:		
Expenditure that is shown in the accounts but is not allowable		
Depreciation		20,000
Employee Loan Written Off		8,000
Increase in General Bad Debt Provision		7,700
Entertaining Customers		9,100
		338,800
Deduct:		
Income that is not taxable as Trading Income		
Rental Income	200,000	
Interest Received from Investments	30,000	
Profit on Sale of Non-current Assets	33,000	
Dividends Received	15,000	
Capital Allowances	153,000	
		(431,000)
Adjusted Trading Loss		(92,200)
Trading Income assessment = zero		

The trading loss of £92,200 could be relieved without carrying it forward (provided the profits are large enough) as follows:

- by offsetting against the taxable total profits (TTP) before deduction of QCD payments in the CAP y/e 31/3/2024, and then if any loss remains

- by offsetting against the taxable total profits (TTP) before deduction of QCD payments arising in the 12 months to 31/3/2023

2.6   The following statement is true: **(b)**

The other statements are false.

CHAPTER 3: CORPORATION TAX – CAPITAL ALLOWANCES

3.1

	Main pool	Capital allowances
	£	£
WDV bf	21,000	
add		
Acquisitions		
without FYA or AIA:		
Car (40 g/km)	16,000	
Acquisitions qualifying for AIA:		
Plant 993,000		
Van 10,000		
————		
1,003,000		
AIA claimed (1,000,000)		1,000,000
————		
	3,000	
less		
Proceeds of Disposals	(2,000)	
————		
	38,000	
18% WDA	(6,840)	6,840
————		
WDV cf	31,160	
————		
Total Capital Allowances		1,006,840

Note that neither the plant nor van qualify for full expensing allowance. The plant and the van are used, not new.

3.2

	Main pool	Capital allowances
	£	£
WDV bf	60,000	
add		
Acquisitions		
without FYA or AIA:		
Car (45 g/km)	24,000	
Acquisitions qualifying for full expensing:		
FL Truck 30,000		
Computer 5,000		
————		
35,000		
100% (35,000)		35,000
————	0	
less		
Proceeds of Disposals:	(3,000)	
	————	
	81,000	
WDA 18%	(14,580)	14,580
Balancing Allowance		
	————	
WDV cf	66,420	
		————
Total Capital Allowances		49,580

Trading Income for CAP year ended 31/3/2024:

	£
Adjusted trading profits	154,000
Plant & Machinery Capital Allowances	(49,580)
	————
Trading Income	104,420

3.3

	Main pool	Special rate pool	Capital allowances
	£	£	£
WDV bf	10,000	2,800	
Acquisitions qualifying for full expensing:			
Plant 1,196,750			
Machinery 12,000			
1,208,750			
Full expensing (1,208,750)			1,208,750
less			
Proceeds of			
Disposals	(3,500)		
	6,500	2,800	
WDA at 18%	(1,170)		1,170
WDA at 6%		(168)	168
WDV cf	5,330	2,632	
Total Capital Allowances			1,210,088

3.4

The CAPs will be:	The AIA limits will be:
1/12/2021 – 30/11/2022 (12 months)	£1,000,000
1/12/2022 – 28/2/2023 (3 months)	£1,000,000 x 3/12 = £250,000

CAP YEAR ENDED 30/11/2022			
	Main pool	Special rate pool	Capital allowances
	£	£	£
WDV bf	60,000	14,000	
add			
Acquisitions			
without FYA or AIA:			
Car (63 g/km)		16,000	
less			
Proceeds of			
Disposals:	(4,000)		
	56,000	30,000	
WDA 18% / 6%	(10,080)	(1,800)	11,880
WDV cf	45,920	28,200	
Total Capital Allowances			11,880

CAP 3 MONTHS ENDED 28/2/2023

		Main pool	Special rate pool	Capital allowances
		£	£	£
WDV bf		45,920	28,200	
Acquisitions qualifying for AIA:				
Plant	45,000			
AIA claimed*	(45,000)			45,000
		0		
		45,920	28,200	
WDA 18% × 3/12		(2,066)		2,066
WDA 6% × 3/12			(423)	423
WDV cf		43,854	27,777	
Total Capital Allowances				47,489

*AIA limit £1,000,000 × 3/12 = £250,000

Calculation of trading income assessments

Time-apportionment of adjusted trade profits:

CAP 1/12/2021 to 30/11/2022	£480,000 × 12/15 = £384,000
CAP 1/12/2022 to 28/2/2023	£480,000 × 3/15 = £96,000

Capital allowances are then deducted from the adjusted profit for each CAP.

	1/12/21 – 30/11/22	1/12/22 – 28/2/23
	£	£
Adjusted profit	384,000	96,000
Capital allowances:	(11,880)	(47,489)
Trading Income	372,120	48,511

3.5 **PLANT & MACHINERY CAPITAL ALLOWANCES COMPUTATION:**

	Main pool	Special rate pool	Capital allowances
	£	£	£
WDV bf	90,000	13,000	
Additions			
without FYA or AIA:			
BMW Car		27,000	
Zero-Emission Car	20,000		
100% FYA	(20,000)	0	20,000
Additions qualifying for full expensing:			
Plant	857,500		
Full expensing*	(857,500)		857,500
Disposals			
Plant	(1,000)		
	89,000	40,000	
WDA 18% × 10/12	(13,350)		13,350
WDA 6% × 10/12		(2,000)	2,000
WDV cf	75,650	38,000	
Total Capital Allowances			892,850

*If AIA had been claimed it would be limited to £833,333

	£
Adjusted trading profit for 10 month CAP to 31/1/2024	1,510,000
less capital allowances	(892,850)
Trading Income assessment	617,150

3.6 SBA claimable in CAP y/e 31/12/2023

(£2,650,000 – £400,000) x 3% x 4/12 = £22,500

SBA claimable in CAP y/e 31/12/2024

(£2,650,000 – £400,000) x 3% = £67,500

CHAPTER 4: CORPORATION TAX – CHARGEABLE GAINS

4.1 Chargeable Assets: **(a), (b), (c), (d), (e).**

Exempt Assets: **(f), (g), (h).**

4.2

	£
Proceeds	1,300,000
less Cost	(600,000)
Unindexed gain	700,000
less Indexation allowance £600,000 × 0.859	(515,400)
Chargeable Gain	184,600
less capital loss brought forward	(15,000)
Chargeable Gain to be brought into the taxable total profits	169,600

4.3

	£
Proceeds	145,000
less Cost	(50,000)
less Indexation £50,000 × 0.729	(36,450)
Chargeable Gain	58,550
less capital loss brought forward	(25,000)
Chargeable Gain to be brought into the taxable total profits	33,550

4.4 **Chargeable Gains**

Factory	£
Proceeds	500,000
less Cost	(300,000)
less Indexation £300,000 × 1.829 (restricted)	(200,000)
	———
Chargeable Gain	nil

The indexation is restricted to avoid turning an unindexed gain into a loss.

4.5 **Chargeable Gain on Shares**

The disposal in January 2000 will be matched with the pool, and deducted from it before the current disposal is dealt with.

FA 1985 Pool Workings

	Number	Cost	Indexed cost
		£	£
1/1/1992 Purchase	3,000	9,000	9,000
Indexation to Jan 1995:			
£9,000 × 0.077			693
1/1/1995 Purchase	12,000	42,000	42,000
	15,000	51,000	51,693
Bonus Shares	3,000		
Indexation to January 2000:			
£51,693 × 0.141			7,289
Balance	18,000	51,000	58,982
1/1/2000 Disposal	(5,000)	(14,167)	(16,384)
Balance	13,000	36,833	42,598
Indexation to December 2017:			
£42,598 × 0.669			28,498
Balance	13,000	36,833	71,096
30/3/2023 Disposal	(10,000)	(28,333)	(54,689)
Balance	3,000	8,500	16,407

Share disposal March 2023:	£
Proceeds	60,000
less cost	(28,333)
less indexation (£54,689 – £28,333)	(26,356)
	————
Chargeable Gain	5,311

4.6

	No. Shares	Cost £	Indexed cost £
Purchase October 2001	5,000	15,500	15,500
Indexation 0.114			1,767
Rights Issue	100	200	200
Subtotal	5,100	15,700	17,467
Indexation 0.534			9,327
Total	5,100	15,700	26,794
Disposal	(5,100)	(15,700)	(26,794)
Pool balance	0	0	0

Proceeds	£45,900
Indexed Cost	£26,794
Gain	£19,106

4.7

	£
Proceeds	1,270,000
less	
Cost	(720,000)
Indexation 720,000 x 0.415	(298,800)
Gain (before rollover relief)	251,200
Rollover relief (deferred gain)	(131,200)
Gain after rollover relief (proceeds not reinvested)	120,000

CHAPTER 5: CORPORATION TAX – CALCULATING THE TAX

5.1 Corporation Tax Computation

	£	£
Adjusted Trading Profits	1,120,000	
less capital allowances – Plant & Machinery	(63,000)	
Trading Income		1,057,000
Property Income		23,000
Interest Receivable		60,000
Chargeable Gains		48,000
less QCD payment		(45,000)
Taxable total profits		1,143,000

	£
Taxable total profits at main rate: £1,143,000 × 25%	285,750

5.2 Corporation Tax Computation

	£	£
Adjusted Trading Profits	1,420,000	
less capital allowances – Plant & Machinery	(205,000)	
Trading Income		1,215,000
Property Income		92,000
Interest Receivable		12,000
Chargeable Gains	88,000	
less capital loss bf	(18,000)	
Net Chargeable Gains		70,000
less QCD payment		(8,000)
Taxable total profits		1,381,000

	£
Taxable total profits at main rate: £1,381,000 × 25%*	345,250

*Upper limit is £250,000/4 = £62,500

5.3   **Corporation Tax Computation**

	£	£
Trading Income		0
Property Income		35,000
Interest Receivable		40,000
Chargeable Gains	90,000	
less capital loss bf	(8,000)	
Net Chargeable Gains		82,000
		157,000
less trading loss		(120,000)
less rental loss bf		(13,000)
less QCD payment		(10,000)
Taxable total profits		14,000

Corporation Tax:

FY 2022: 3/12 x £14,000 = £3,500 x main rate 19% =	£665
FY 2023: 9/12 x £14,000 = £10,500 x small profits rate* 19% =	£1,995
Total	£2,660

*Lower limit is £50,000 x 9/12 = £37,500

An alternative option would be to carry the loss forward against future taxable total profits.

5.4

	£	£
Net Profit per accounts		251,000
Add Back:		
Expenditure that is shown in the accounts but is not allowable:		
Depreciation		41,000
Directors' Speeding Fines		1,000
Gifts of Food (Hampers)		10,000
Entertaining Customers		6,000
		309,000
Deduct:		
Income that is not taxable as trading income:		
Interest Receivable	50,000	
Profit on Disposal of Non-current Assets	50,000	
Rental Income Receivable	40,000	
Capital Allowances	11,000	
		(151,000)
Trading Income Assessment		158,000

Corporation Tax Computation

	£
Trading Income	158,000
Property Income	40,000
Interest Receivable	50,000
Chargeable Gains	41,000
Taxable total profits	289,000
Corporation Tax at main rate: £289,000 × 25%	£72,250

5.5

	£
Net Profit for 16-month period per accounts	4,070
Add back non-allowable expenditure:	
Depreciation etc	10,000
Entertaining customers	1,930
Adjusted profit before capital allowances	16,000

Time-apportionment of adjusted profit:

CAP 1/4/2022 to 31/3/2023 £16,000 × 12/16 = £12,000

CAP 1/4/2023 to 31/7/2023 £16,000 × 4/16 = £4,000

Deduction of Capital Allowances:

	1/4/2022 to 31/3/2023	1/4/2023 to 31/7/2023
	£	£
Adjusted profit	12,000	4,000
Capital allowances	(8,000)	(2,500)
Trading Income	4,000	1,500

Corporation Tax Computation – CAP 1/4/2022 to 31/3/2023

	£
Trading Income	4,000
Taxable total profits	4,000
Corporation Tax at Main Rate: £4,000 × 19%	£760

Corporation Tax Computation – CAP 1/4/2023 to 31/7/2023

	£
Trading Income	1,500
Chargeable Gains	45,000
Taxable total profits	46,500
Corporation Tax at main rate:	
£46,500 × 25%	£11,625
less marginal relief 3/200 x (83,333 – 46,500)	£(552)
Corporating Tax	£11,073

5.6 The following statements are true: **(a), (c), (d).**

CHAPTER 6: INCOME TAX – TRADING PROFITS

6.1 **Profit motive**. Michelle seems to deliberately buy and sell at a profit. She buys property in need of renovation, and times the sale to obtain most profit. This indicates trading.

Subject matter. Michelle gets personal use from the properties that she buys, and this could indicate that she is not trading. She could argue that she is simply changing homes like most people.

Length of ownership. After renovating the buildings, Michelle only keeps them for a few months. Such a short time indicates trading.

Frequency of transactions. The buying and selling of property seems to be quite a regular activity, although with each transaction spaced nearly a year apart it could be argued that it is not particularly frequent.

Supplementary work. Renovating the properties counts as supplementary work, and this is clearly carried out with a view to a future sale.

Reason for acquisition and sale. Although the first property was bequeathed to her, she seems to have subsequently bought with the ultimate sale in mind. This indicates trading.

Source of finance. Since Michelle finances both the purchases and renovations with short-term bank loans, this implies that she intends to sell quickly to repay the money. This points to trading. If the properties had been purchased with long-term mortgages, she could have argued that she had originally intended to keep them for longer.

6.2

1	add back (disallowable expense)
2	add back (disallowable expense)
3	deduct (not trading income)
4	deduct (not trading income)
5	add back (disallowable expense)
6	deduct (not taxable income)
7	add back (disallowable expense)
8	add back (disallowable expense since food)
9	no action (taxable trading income)
10	add back (disallowable expense – part of drawings)
11	no action (allowable)
12	add back (disallowable expense)

6.3

	£	£
Net Profit per accounts		144,000
Add Back:		
Expenditure that is shown in the accounts but is not allowable		
Drawings		18,000
Depreciation		22,000
Loss on Sale of Non-current Assets		4,000
Gift Vouchers		3,000
Entertaining Customers		4,500
Owner's Pension Contribution		2,400
		———
		197,900
Deduct:		
Income that is not taxable as trading income		
Interest Received	12,000	
Rental Income	10,000	
Capital Allowances	23,000	
	———	
		(45,000)
		———
Trading Income Assessment		152,900
		———

6.4 **The capital allowance computation is as follows:**

The following acquisitions qualify for AIA:

Computer System	£2,000
Shop Counter	£3,000
Total	£5,000 (below AIA limit)

	£	Main pool £	Single asset pool car (40% private) £	Capital allowances £
WDV bf		25,000	10,000	
Additions with FYAs:				
Zero-emission car	26,000			
FYA (100%)	(26,000) × 60%			15,600
Acquisitions qualifying for AIA:				
Computer	2,000			
Shop Counter	3,000			
AIA claimed	(5,000)	0		5,000
Disposals:				
Private use car			(4,000)	
Food Processor		(200)		
Sub totals		24,800	6,000	
WDA 18%		(4,464)		4,464
Balancing Allowance			(6,000) × 60%	3,600
WDV cf		20,336	–	
Total Capital Allowances				28,664

Calculation of Adjusted Profit (Loss):

	£
Adjusted trading profits (before capital allowances)	12,000
Capital allowances (as above)	(28,664)
Loss	(16,664)

The trading income assessment for 2023/24 is nil.

6.5 There is no AIA claimable.

Plant & Machinery Capital Allowances Computation

	Main pool	Car 20% private BMW	Special rate 20% private Range Rover	Capital allowances
Single Asset Pools				
	£	£	£	£
WDV bf	66,300	16,000	–	
Additions				
without FYA or AIA:				
Range Rover			28,000	
(200 g/km)				
Ford	19,000			
(40 g/km)				
Disposals:				
BMW		(12,000)		
Vauxhall	(4,000)			
	———	———	———	
	81,300	4,000	28,000	
WDA 18%	(14,634)			14,634
WDA 6%			(1,680) × 80%	1,344
Balancing Allowance		(4,000) × 80%		3,200
	———	———	———	
WDV cf	66,666	–	26,320	
				———
Total Capital Allowances				19,178
				———

Adjustment of Trading Profits:

	£	£
Net Profit per accounts		110,000
Add Back:		
Expenditure that is shown in the accounts but is not allowable		
Drawings		45,000
Depreciation		38,000
Loss on Sale of BMW		3,000
Entertaining Customers		2,000
		———
		198,000

Deduct:

Income that is not taxable as trading income

	Reduction in general bad debt provision	4,000	
	Gain on Sale of Vauxhall	1,000	
Capital Allowances – Plant & Machinery		19,178	
			(24,178)
	Trading Income Assessment		173,822

6.6

	£	£
Net loss		(3,785)
Add		
Depreciation	28,019	
Mr Chang's salary	30,000	
Gifts to customers	2,250	
Subscription to golf club	220	
Motor expenses for Mr Chang's car	5,700	
	66,189	
		62,404
less		
Capital allowances		9,878
Adjusted trading profits		52,526

CHAPTER 7: INCOME TAX – FURTHER ISSUES

7.1 Using the general options, Louise could

- Set the loss against the trading income of £20,000 for 2024/25 and carry the remaining £10,000 loss forward against the next trading profits. This will waste the personal allowance for 2024/25.

- Set the loss against the total income of £14,000 for 2022/23, and set the remaining £16,000 loss against the trading income of £20,000 for 2024/25. This will waste all the personal allowance in 2022/23, and part of the personal allowance in 2024/25.

Using the opening years loss provision, Louise could

- Set the entire loss against the total income of £65,000 in 2020/21. This will give tax relief partly at the higher rate, and it will not waste any personal allowances. The cash flow benefit of the loss relief will come in the form of a tax refund for 2020/21.

- It is recommended that the opening years provision should be used to offset the loss against total income of 2020/21.

7.2 By using the general loss provisions of current year plus carry-back, John could set his loss against the **total income** of 2022/23 and/or 2023/24.

- Setting against 2022/23 only would leave income of only £1,000 for that year, so would waste the majority of the personal allowance for that year.

- Setting against 2023/24, followed by 2022/23, would waste the personal allowance for 2023/24.

By using the terminal loss option, John could set against **trading income** in 2022/23, followed by 2021/22. This would reduce his total income in 2022/23 to £12,000 (just the 'other income'). It would leave £25,000 - £14,000 = £11,000 loss to be set against trading income in 2021/22, so total income that year would be £20,000 - £11,000 + £12,000 = £21,000. There would be minimal wastage of the personal allowance in any year.

Using the terminal loss option is recommended. The figures would then appear as follows:

	2020/21 £	2021/22 £	2022/23 £	2023/24 £
Trading income	35,000	20,000	14,000	0
Terminal loss relief		(11,000)	(14,000)	
Other income	12,000	12,000	12,000	12,000
Total income	47,000	21,000	12,000	12,000

7.3 The accounting year to 31/12/2022 profits of £96,000 will need to be time-apportioned before dividing them amongst the partners:

1/1/2022 – 30/9/2022	9/12 × £96,000 = £72,000
Alice (50%)	£36,000
Bob (50%)	£36,000

1/10/2022 – 31/12/2022	3/12 × £96,000 = £24,000
Alice (45%)	£10,800
Bob (40%)	£9,600
Colin (15%)	£3,600

The accounting year to 31/12/2023 profits of £108,000 are divided as follows:

Alice (45%)	£48,600
Bob (40%)	£43,200
Colin (15%)	£16,200

7.4 **Capital Allowances:**

Plant & Machinery

	Main pool	Single asset pool car (30% private)	Capital allowances
	£	£	£
WDV bf	35,000	16,000	
Disposal:			
Car		(10,000)	
WDA 18%	(6,300)		6,300
Balancing Allowance		(6,000) × 70%	4,200
WDV cf	28,700	0	–
Total Capital Allowances			10,500

Adjustment of Profits

	£	£
Net Profit per accounts		71,000
Add Back:		
Expenditure that is shown in the accounts but is not allowable		
Depreciation		12,250
Private motor expenses		500
Increase in General Provision for Bad Debts		200
Gift Vouchers for customers		400
		84,350
Deduct:		
Allowable expenditure not shown in accounts		
Plant & Machinery Capital Allowances	10,500	
		(10,500)
Adjusted Profits for y/e 31/3/2024		73,850

Trading Income assessment for Olga for 2023/24

This is her last tax year for the business.

Her share of the adjusted profits is: £73,850 × 1/3 = £24,617

Trading Income assessment   £24,617

Class 4 National Insurance

This is calculated based on the trading income figure.

9% of (£24,617 – £12,750) = £1,084.23

7.5

	£	£
Net profit per accounts		21,500
add disallowable expenditure		
Private van running costs		1,260
Depreciation		2,800
Entertaining		1,000
Private telephone and postage		200
		26,760
less allowable expenditure		
Heating and lighting office	150	
Capital allowances	4,200	
		(4,350)
Adjusted profit		22,410

7.6   Only **(c)** is true; the rest are false

7.7

	Monica £	Norman £	Olga £	Paula £	Total £
Period to 31 May					
Salary	27,000	27,000	36,000		90,000
Interest on capital	13,500	7,200	16,200		36,900
Profit Share	129,240	64,620	129,240		323,100
Total	169,740	98,820	181,440		450,000
Period to 31 August					
Salary	9,000		12,000	6,000	27,000
Interest on capital	4,500		5,400	1,800	11,700
Profit Share	33,390		44,520	33,390	111,300
Total	46,890		61,920	41,190	150,000
Total for year	216,630	98,820	243,360	41,190	600,000

CHAPTER 8: BUSINESS DISPOSALS AND TAX PLANNING

8.1 **(a)** Exempt

 (b) Exempt

 (c) Chargeable

 (d) Chargeable

 (e) Chargeable

 (f) Chargeable

 (g) Exempt

 (h) Exempt

8.2

		£
(a)	Proceeds	140,000
	less cost	(60,000)
	Gain	80,000
	less annual exempt amount	(6,000)
	Amount subject to CGT	74,000
	Capital Gains Tax £74,000 × 20% =	14,800

		£
(b)	Gain	80,000
	less annual exempt amount	(6,000)
	Amount subject to CGT	74,000
	Capital Gains Tax £74,000 × 10% =	7,400

8.3 **(a)** Amount of William's gain:

	£	£
Proceeds		200,000
less market value when received	100,000	
minus deferred gain	(33,160)	
		(66,840)
Gain		133,160
less annual exempt amount		(6,000)
Amount subject to CGT		127,160
Capital Gains Tax £127,160 × 20% =		25,432

(b)

	£
Gain	133,160
less annual exempt amount	(6,000)
Amount subject to CGT	127,160
Capital Gains Tax £127,160 × 10% =	12,716

8.4 The first step is to allocate the sale proceeds to the individual assets, and determine which assets are chargeable.

	£	
Premises	1,700,000	Chargeable
Plant & Machinery	20,000	Proceeds < Cost. Dealt with through capital allowance computation
Net Current Assets	50,000	Exempt
Goodwill	130,000	Chargeable
Total Proceeds	1,900,000	

The goodwill is calculated as the balancing figure, after accounting for the other assets.

The computations are then carried out individually on the chargeable assets.

	£	£
Premises		
Proceeds		1,700,000
less Cost		(340,000)
Gain		1,360,000
Goodwill		
Proceeds		130,000
less Cost		0
Gain		130,000

Summary	£
Gain on premises	1,360,000
Gain on goodwill	130,000
Total Gains	1,490,000
less Annual Exempt Amount	(6,000)
Amount subject to CGT	1,484,000
	100,000
CGT £1,000,000 × 10%	
£484,000 x 20%	96,800
Total CGT	196,800

8.5 **(c)** When a capital loss made by an individual is offset against gains in the following tax year, it is only to the extent that it reduces those gains to the amount of the annual exemption

8.6 **(b)** Gain = £300,000

less annual exempt amount £6,000 = £294,000

Taxed at 10% = £29,400.

8.7 **(a)**

Expenditure	Tax-deductible	Not tax-deductible
Drawings of sole trader		✔
Agreed salary of sole trader's spouse	✔	
Salaries of partners		✔
Salary of sole trader		✔

(b)

Expenditure	Tax-deductible	Not tax-deductible
Dividends		✔
Agreed salary of shareholder's spouse	✔	
Salaries of directors	✔	

8.8   Option 1: The salary plus employers NIC (although the employment allowance could be claimed against employers NIC) would be tax-deductible for the business, so this would reduce David's taxable income, and he would become a basic rate taxpayer instead of the current higher rate. It would also reduce slightly David's Class 4 NIC liability (mainly the 2% level). Sue would utilise her personal allowance, and the remainder of her salary would be taxed at basic rate. She would pay employees NIC. Her Income Tax and NIC would be deducted through PAYE.

Option 2: The change to a partnership would share the existing profits, and Sue would receive a similar amount to the alternative salary. David's taxable income would be reduced, and he would become a basic rate taxpayer. It would also reduce David's Class 4 NIC slightly, mainly at the 2% rate. Sue would utilise her personal allowance, and she would pay basic rate tax and Class 2 and Class 4 NIC through the self-assessment system, with the final payment date 31 January following the end of the tax year.

Reference Material

For AAT Assessment of Business Tax
Finance Act 2023

For assessments from 29 January 2024

Note: This reference material is accessible by candidates during their live computer based assessment for Business Tax.

This material was current at the time this book was published, but may be subject to change. Readers are advised to check the AAT website or Osborne Books website for any updates.

Reference material for AAT assessment of Business Tax

Introduction

This document comprises data that you may need to consult during your Business Tax computer-based assessment.

The material can be consulted during the practice and live assessments by using the reference materials section at each task position. It's made available here so you can familiarise yourself with the content before the assessment.

Do not take a print of this document into the exam room with you*.

This document may be changed to reflect periodical updates in the computer-based assessment, so please check you have the most recent version while studying. This version is based on **Finance Act 2023** and is for use in AAT Q2022 assessments from **29 January 2024**

*Unless you need a printed version as part of reasonable adjustments for particular needs, in which case you must discuss this with your tutor at least six weeks before the assessment date.

> Note that page numbers refer to those in the original AAT Guidance document

Contents

1. Income tax

Trading allowance			£1,000
Personal allowance			£12,570
	Basic rate (0-£37,700)	Higher rate (£37,701 - £125,140)	Additional rate (Above £125,140)
Salary	20%	40%	45%
Dividends	8.75%	33.75%	39.35%
Trading income	20%	40%	45%

- Income tax computations will not be required in the assessment, but the rates may be used in tax planning discussions.

2. National Insurance (NI)

Class 2 contributions	£3.45 per week
Lower profits threshold	£12,570
Class 4 contributions on trading profits between £12,570 and £50,270	9%
Class 4 contributions on trading profits above £50,270	2%

- Dividends are not subject to NI
- Salaries are subject to:
  - employee NI at 12% between £12,570 and £50,270 and 2% above £50,270
  - employer NI at 13.8% above £9,100 (an employment allowance of £5,000 is available)

  Calculations of NI on salaries will not be required in the assessment but the rates may be used in tax planning discussions

3. Capital gains tax

Annual exempt amount	£6,000
Basic rate	10%
Higher rate	20%
Business asset disposal relief rate	10%
Business asset disposal relief lifetime allowance	£1,000,000

4. Corporation tax

Rate of corporation tax prior to 1 April 2023	19%
Main rate of corporation tax from 1 April 2023	25%
Small profits rate of corporation tax from 1 April 2023	19%
Upper limit	£250,000*
Lower limit	£50,000*
Marginal small company relief	3/200 x (upper limit -TTP)

*reduced if:
- accounting period <12 months
- associated companies.

5. Capital allowances

Assets other than cars:	
Annual investment allowance	£1,000,000
Writing down allowance	18%
Full expensing – expenditure by companies after 1 April 2023	100%

Cars:	
Writing down allowance:	
- CO2 emissions 0g/km	100%
- CO2 emissions up to 50 g/km	18%
- CO2 emissions over 50 g/km	6%

Small pools allowance	£1,000
Structures and buildings allowance	3%

6.   Disallowed expenditure

Type of expense	Disallowable in calculation of trading profit	Notes
Fines and penalties	Fines on the business Fines on directors/owners	Employee fines are not disallowed if incurred in the course of their employment.
Donations	Political donations Donations to national charities	Donations to local charities are allowable (these will only be examined for unincorporated businesses).
Capital expenditure	Depreciation Loss on disposal Capital items expensed	Capital allowances may be available.
Legal and professional	Relating to: - capital items - purchase/renewal of a long lease - purchase of a short lease (50 years or less) - breaches of law/regulations.	Legal fees on the renewal of a short lease (50 years or less) are allowable.
Entertaining and gifts	Customer gifts (unless <£50 per annum, not food, drink, tobacco, or cash vouchers and contains business advertising). Customer/supplier entertaining.	Staff gifts and staff entertaining are allowable.
Cars	Depreciation. Private use by owners. 15% of lease cost if leased car >50g/km CO2 emissions.	
Private expenditure of owner (unincorporated businesses only)	Goods taken for own use. Salary of owners. Private use % by owners. Private expenditure, e.g., Class 2 and 4 NICs, legal and professional fees for personal expenditure.	Reasonable salaries of family members are allowable.

7. Trading losses

Loss option	Sole trader/Partner	Company
Carry forward	Against future profits of the same trade only. Applies automatically to first available profits. Applies after any other elections or if no elections are made.	Losses not relieved in the current accounting period or previous 12 months are carried forward and an election can be made to set against total profits in future periods.
Current year/carry back	Against total income in the current and/or previous tax year in any order. If opted for in either year, the amount of loss used cannot be restricted to preserve the personal allowance. Make claim by 31 January 2026 for 2023/24 tax year.	Can elect to set trading losses against current accounting period 'total profits'. Qualifying charitable donations will remain unrelieved. If the above election is made, can also carry back trading loss to set against 'total profits' within the previous 12 months. Claim within 2 years of the end of the loss-making period.
Opening year loss relief – loss in first four years of trade	Against total income of the previous three tax years on a FIFO basis. If opted for, losses will be used to reduce total income as much as possible in each year and cannot be restricted to preserve the personal allowance. Make claim by 31 January 2026 for 2023/24 tax year.	N/A
Terminal loss relief	Against trading profits of the previous 3 years on a LIFO basis. Claim within 4 years from the end of the last tax year of trade.	Against total profits of the previous 3 years. Claim within 2 years of the end of the loss-making period.

8.   Chargeable gains – Reliefs

Relief	Conditions
Replacement of business assets (Rollover) relief	Available to individuals and companies. Examinable for companies. Qualifying assets (original and replacement) – must be used in a trade and be land and buildings or fixed plant and machinery. Qualifying time period – replacement asset must be purchased between one year before and three years after the sale of the original asset. Partial reinvestment – if only some of the sales proceeds reinvested then the gain taxable is the lower of the full gain and the proceeds not reinvested.
Gift relief (holdover relief)	Available to individuals only. Qualifying assets – assets used in the trade of the donor or the donor's personal company, shares in any unquoted trading company or shares in the donors personal trading company. A personal trading company is one where the donor has at least 5%.
Business asset disposal relief	Available to individuals only. Gain taxable at 10%. £1m lifetime limit For 2023/24 a claim must be made by 31 January 2026. Qualifying assets: - the whole or part of a business carried on by the individual (alone or in partnership). The business must have been owned for 24 months prior to sale - assets of the individual's or partnership's trading business that has now ceased. The business must have been owned for 24 months prior to cessation and sale must be within 3 years of cessation - shares in the individual's 'personal trading company' (own at least 5%). The individual must have owned the shares and been an employee of the company for 24 months prior to sale.

9. Payment and administration

	Sole traders/partners	Company
Filing date	31 October following the end of the tax year if filing a paper return. 31 January following the end of the tax year if filing online. Amendments can be made within 12 months of the filing deadline.	Filed on the later of 12 months after end of AP or 3 months after the notice to deliver a tax return has been issued. Amendments can be made within 12 months of the filing deadline.
Payment date	31 January following the end of the tax year. If payments on accounts are due: • first POA – 31 January during tax year • second POA – 31 July after tax year • balancing payment – 31 January after tax year. POA's are each 50% of the previous years income tax and class 4 NICS due by self-assessment. POA's are not required for capital gains or class 2 NICs. POA's are not due if prior year tax payable by self-assessment is less than £1,000 OR if >80% of prior year tax was collected at source.	Small companies (annual profits less than £1.5 million): 9 months + 1 day after end of the accounting period (AP). Large companies (annual profits greater than £1.5 million) must estimate the year's tax liability and pay 25% of the estimate on the 14th day of each of the 7th, 10th, 13th and 16th month from the start of the accounting period.
Interest	Charged daily on late payment	Interest charged daily on late payment. Overpayment of tax receives interest from HMRC. Interest is taxable/tax allowable as interest income.
Penalties for late filing	£100. After 3 months, £10 per day for up to 90 days. After 6 months, 5% tax due (or £300 if greater). After 12 months, 5% tax due (or £300 if greater) if not deliberate. After 12 months, 70% of tax due (or £300 if greater) if deliberate and not concealed. After 12 months, 100% tax due (or £300 if greater) if deliberate and concealed.	£100. After 3 months, £100. After 6 months, 10% of unpaid tax. After 12 months, 10% of unpaid tax.
Late payment	30 days late – 5% of tax outstanding at that date. 6 months days late – 5% of tax outstanding at that date. 12 months late – 5% of tax outstanding at that date.	N/A

Notify of chargeability	5 October following the end of the tax year.	Within 3 months of starting to trade.
	Sole traders/partners	**Company**
Enquiry	Within 12 months of submission of return. Penalty for failure to produce enquiry documents = £300 + £60 per day.	Within 12 months of submission of return. Penalty for failure to produce enquiry documents: £300 + £60 per day.
Record retention	Five years from filing date. Penalty for failure to keep records is up to £3,000.	Six years after the end of the relevant accounting period. Penalty for failure to keep proper records is up to £3,000.

10. Penalties for incorrect returns

Type of behaviour	Maximum	Unprompted (minimum)	Prompted (minimum
Careless error and inaccuracy are due to failure to take reasonable care	30%	0%	15%
Deliberate error but not concealed	70%	20%	35%
Deliberate error and concealed	100%	30%	50%

Index

for your notes

for your notes

for your notes

for your notes

for your notes

for your notes

for your notes

for your notes

for your notes

for your notes

for your notes